Integral Faith Education of Adolescents and Youth

Based on the Principle of Graduality

A Guide for Youth Ministers, Teachers, Catechists and Parents

Gatien Ngah

ISBN 979-8-88943-456-6 (paperback)
ISBN 979-8-88943-457-3 (digital)

Copyright © 2023 by Gatien Ngah

All rights reserved. No part of this publication may be reproduced, distributed, or transmitted in any form or by any means, including photocopying, recording, or other electronic or mechanical methods without the prior written permission of the publisher. For permission requests, solicit the publisher via the address below.

Christian Faith Publishing
832 Park Avenue
Meadville, PA 16335
www.christianfaithpublishing.com

Printed in the United States of America

CONTENTS

ABBREVIATIONS vii
FOREWORD ix
PREFACE xi
ACKNOWLEDGMENTS xiii
INTRODUCTION xv

CHAPTER 1: UNDERSTANDING ADOLESCENCE AND YOUTH 1
  1.1. Definition 1
  1.2. Stages of Adolescence 3
    1.2.1. Early Adolescence: Ages 10 to 13 3
      1.2.1.1. Physical Development 3
      1.2.1.2. Cognitive and Emotional Development 4
    1.2.2. Middle Adolescence: Ages 14 to 17 5
      1.2.2.1. Physical Development 5
      1.2.2.2. Cognitive and Emotional Development 5
    1.2.3. Late Adolescence: Ages 18 to 21 6
      1.2.3.1. Physical Development 6
      1.2.3.2. Cognitive and Emotional Development 7
  1.3. Youth 8

CHAPTER 2: UNDERSTANDING THE PRINCIPLE OF GRADUALITY 11
  2.1. Definition 11
  2.2. The Principle of Graduality in Moral Theology 11
  2.3. The Principle of Graduality in Pedagogy 14
    2.3.1. The Three Domains of Learning 15
      2.3.1.1. Cognitive Domain 17

  2.3.1.2. Affective Domain 18
  2.3.1.3. Behavioral Domain 19
 2.4. The Principle of Graduality in the *Directory*
 ** *for Catechesis*** 20
  2.4.1. Pathways of Catechesis 20
  2.4.2. Catechesis in the World of Young People 21

CHAPTER 3: UNDERSTANDING INTEGRAL FAITH EDUCATION 23
 3.1. Integral Dimensions of Faith Education 23
  3.1.1. Spiritual Dimension 24
  3.1.2. Human Dimension 24
  3.1.3. Intellectual Dimension 25
  3.1.4. Apostolic Dimension 26
 3.2. Perspectives of Integral Faith Education 27
  3.2.1. Faith as Believing 27
  3.2.2. Faith as Trusting 30
  3.2.3. Faith as Doing 31

CHAPTER 4: CATECHESIS OF ADOLESCENTS AND YOUTH 33
 4.1. Theoretical Considerations 33
  4.1.1. Psychosocial Perspective of Adolescents 33
  4.1.2. The Application of the Principle of Graduality ...36
  4.1.3. Catechetical Consideration for Adolescents 38
  4.1.4. Catechetical Consideration for Youth 43
  4.1.5. Youth Culture and Popular Youth Ministry 45
 4.2. Operational Considerations 46
  4.2.1. The Principle of Graduality and
   Communication of the Faith to Adolescents 47
   4.2.1.1. Guidelines of Effective Faith
    Communication 47
   4.2.1.2. Guidelines on the Language of Young People 49
   4.2.1.3. Guidelines from the "Principle of
    Graduality" in the Adolescence Life of Jesus 52

CHAPTER 5: GOALS AND TASKS OF FAITH EDUCATION OF ADOLESCENTS AND YOUTH..........55
5.1. Goals of Faith Education..........55
   1.1.1. Communion with Jesus Christ..........55
   1.1.2. Integral Formation..........56
   1.1.3. Conversion..........56
   1.1.4. Confession of Faith in the One God..........57
1.2. Tasks of Faith Education..........57
   5.2.1. Promoting Knowledge of the Faith..........57
   5.2.2. Liturgical Education..........58
   5.2.3. Moral Formation..........58
   5.2.4. Teaching to Pray..........59
   5.2.5. Education for Community Life..........59
   5.2.6. Missionary Initiation..........60
5.3. Faith-Focused Mentoring as a Holistic Process for Adolescents and Youth..........60

CHAPTER 6: THE STRATEGY OF THE CHURCH IN MINISTERING TO ADOLESCENTS AND YOUTH..........63
6.1. Pastoral Strategy..........63
6.2. Organic and Structured Catechetical Programs..........65
6.3. Casual Catechetical or Educational Programs..........66
6.4. Vocational Dimension of Adolescence and Youth Catechesis..........66
6.5. Some Other Strategies for Adolescents and Youth Faith Education..........67
   6.5.1. Use of Arts in Catechesis..........68
   6.5.2. Music and Catechesis..........69
   6.5.3. Comedy and Catechesis..........71
   6.5.4. Movies/Stories and Catechesis..........72
   6.5.5. Use of Cartoons/Comics in Catechesis..........73

CHAPTER 7: WORLD YOUTH DAY AS A PASTORAL GUIDE FOR EVERY YOUTH MINISTRY..........75
7.1. The Importance of World Youth Day..........75
   7.1.1. WYD as a Festival of Faith..........78

7.1.2. Experience of the Church 78
7.1.3. Missionary Experience 79
7.1.4. Vocational Discernment and Call to Holiness 80
7.1.5. Experience of Pilgrimage 81
7.1.6. Universal Fraternity 82
7.2. Cooperation with Youth Leaders 83
7.3. Icons of WYD 83
 7.3.1. WYD Cross 83
 7.3.2. WYD Icon 84
7.4. Message of the WYD 84
7.5. Youth Festival 85
7.6. Pastoral Guide for Youth Ministry 86

CHAPTER 8: THE NECESSITY OF SUITABLE ENVIRONMENTS
    FOR ADOLESCENTS AND YOUTH 87
8.1. The Priority of the Pastoral Care of Young People 87
8.2. What Is a Youth Center or Oratory Meant For? 89
8.3. Testimony and Way Forward 90
 8.1.1. The Role of the Community 93
 8.1.2. Qualities of Youth Ministers 93
 8.1.3. Two Main Courses of Action in the Youth
   Ministry 95

CONCLUSION 101
BIBLIOGRAPHY 107
APPENDIX: SUMMARY OF KEY AREAS 111

ABBREVIATIONS

DC—*Directory for Catechesis* (2020)
GCD—*General Catechetical Directory* (1971)
CCC—*Catechism of the Catholic Church* (1992)
CT—*Catechesi Tradendae: Apostolic Exhortation on Catechesis Today* (1979)
ChV—*Christus Vivit: Post-Synodal Apostolic Exhortation to Young People and to the Entire People of God* (2019)
EA—*Ecclesia in Africa, Post-Synodal Apostolic Exhortation, On the Church in Africa and Its Evangelizing Mission Towards the Year 2000* (1995)
EG—*Evangelii Gaudium: Apostolic Exhortation on the Proclamation of the Gospel in Today's World* (2013)
FC—*Familiaris Consortio: Apostolic Exhortation on the Role of Christian Family in the Modern World* (1981)
GE—*Gaudete et Exsultate: Apostolic Exhortation on the Call to Holiness in Today's World* (2018)
WYD—World Youth Day

FOREWORD

As a participant of the Fifteenth Ordinary General Assembly of the Synod of Bishops on *Young People, the Faith and Vocational Discernment*, which took place from October 3 to 28, 2018, one of the emphases was on the integral faith education of the young. Many concrete proposals emerged for the renewing of the pastoral care of young people, freeing it from approaches that are no longer effective because they are incapable of entering into dialogue with contemporary youth culture (*Cf. ChV. n. 208*). This research work on the *Integral Faith Education of Adolescents and Youth: Based on the Principle of Graduality* comes to answer one of the needs (integral faith education) of the pastoral care of the young in this generation. It makes use of the magisterial documents (along with other sources) pertaining to the pastoral care of young people such as *Christus Vivit (2019), Directory for Catechesis (2020),* and *Pastoral Guidelines for the Celebration of World Youth Day in the Particular Churches (2021).*

I, therefore, append my voice once again to that of the Synod Fathers that the pastoral care of the young needs to be *synodal*. Young people themselves are agents of youth ministry and need to be listened to, understood, loved, and accompanied. In as much as they need to be helped and guided, at the same time, they need to be left free to develop new approaches, with creativity and a certain audacity (*Cf. ChV. n. 203*). This work is a contribution to enlighten youth ministers, teachers, catechists, and parents to assist the young integrally in the *synodal* process according to their age groups so that they can better profess their faith, celebrate their faith, pray their faith, and translate their faith into the various aspects of their lives in the Church and the society.

May the objectives of this work be realized, through the intercession of Saint John Bosco and Pope Saint John Paul II, in the life and ministry of youth workers, the young people, and the entire Church.

—+Andrew Fuanya Nkea
Archbishop of Bamenda, Cameroon, Africa
President of the National Episcopal Conference of Cameroon
January 31, 2023, Feast of Saint John Bosco

PREFACE

Education of the young is a primary, crucial, and fundamental task of a faith community. An integral youth ministry, as *Christus Vivit* presents it, is basically an integral education of the young (*Christus Vivit*, 247) for their own sakes and the sake of the community toward fraternity and social friendship (*Fratelli tutti*, 114). The young are the hope and wealth of every community. As I congratulate Fr. Gatien Ngah for his effort in bringing out this material as a book, I wish him all success in his pastoral ministry, especially with the young, in educating them and accompanying them in their maturity into the complete persons that they are called to be.

This work is a pertinent reminder about the importance of the principle of graduality that takes persons as they are and values them for what they are, challenging them to grow fully toward who they are—sons and daughters of the Lord of life!

The book follows an approach that begins with the psychosocial and pedagogical background of knowledge that is available and looks for a catechetical pedagogy adept for educating adolescents and youths. In simple words, it uses as its point of departure and as a determining factor the concrete reality, the growth process, problems, and the events which have a decisive role in defining the faith experience of the young that their further education would augur within each of them a genuine and efficacious conversion. The book takes seriously the aspect of the twofold fidelity—fidelity to God and fidelity to humanity—with a judicious synthesis of the anthropological and theological dimensions of life and faith of the young (*Directory for Catechesis*, 179).

Certainly, this work can be recommended to the youth ministers, catechists, teachers, and parents who deal with adolescents and youths so that it could inspire them in eliciting a positive response from the young placed in their care. The book could be a valuable academic tool for every person and institution entrusted with the pastoral care of the young.

May the dream of this work, offering integral faith education to the young, come true in every community of faith that is reached out to, in, and through this work.

—Antony Christy Lourdunathan
Associate Professor, Institute of Catechetics,
Pontifical Salesian University (UPS), Rome

ACKNOWLEDGMENTS

Gratitude to the following persons for their contributions to the realization of this work:

- *Most Reverend Dr. Andrew Fuanya Nkea (Archbishop of Bamenda)*
- *Prof. Antony Christy Lourdunathan (Institute of Catechetics, UPS, Rome)*
- *Prof. Luciano Meddi (Institute of Missiology, PUU, Rome)*
- *Fr. Paul Remjika (Doctoral Student, Canon Law)*
- *Fr. Samuel Tabeson (Doctoral Student, Biblical Theology)*
- *Mgr. Cornelius Fontem Esua (Archbishop Emeritus of Bamenda)*
- *Dicastery for Evangelization, Rome*
- *Ms. Beldrine Nti (cover page designer)*
- *ALL the authors of the books and the magisterial documents consulted*
- *ALL adolescents, youths, youth ministers, pastors, and faith formation coordinators consulted in the various Parishes during the research program*

God bless you!

INTRODUCTION

Pope Saint John Paul II exhorted the Church in Africa in the following words:

> The *pastoral care of youth* must clearly be a part of the overall pastoral plan of Dioceses and Parishes, so that young people will be enabled to discover very early on the value of the gift of self, an essential means for the person to reach maturity.[1]

This maturity can best be reached through integral faith education, especially that of adolescents and youth beginning from their early stages of growth. The Pontiff further admonished in this regard that "in Africa today[,] formation in the faith too often stops at the elementary stage, and the sects easily profit from this ignorance. A serious deepening of the faith is thus urgently needed."[2] The question, therefore, is, What do we understand by this deepening of the faith, and what method can best fit the faith education of adolescents and youth?

Deepening of faith, or in other words, *catechesis*, is education in the faith of children, young people, and adults that includes especially

---

[1] JOHN PAUL II, Post-Synodal Apostolic Exhortation *Ecclesia in Africa. On the Church in Africa and its Evangelizing Mission Towards the Year 2000*, Liberia Editrice Vaticana, Vatican City 1995, n. 93. Hence, shall be quoted as EA.
[2] *EA*, n. 76.

the teaching of Christian doctrine imparted, generally speaking, in an organic and systematic way, with a view of initiating the hearers into the fullness of Christian life.³ In this regard, it can be said that it is a lifelong process of initial conversion, formation, education, and ongoing conversion. This is done through word, worship, service, and community. It seeks to lead all of God's people to an ever-deepening relationship with God who reveals himself in Jesus Christ through the power of the Holy Spirit. With this understanding, catechesis, therefore, is an educational activity directed toward the total person, which includes one's knowledge, attitudes, values, and skills. This implies that catechesis of adolescents and youth should always target their total personality geared toward guidance in knowledge and practice of the faith, good attitudes to cultivate, human and moral values to be learned and lived, and finally, skills that will help in living the faith and a suitable happy life in the society.

Motivation

During my five years of ministry as diocesan youth chaplain of the Archdiocese of Bamenda (Cameroon, Africa) and two years as provincial episcopal secretary for the commission of youth affairs in the Bamenda Provincial Episcopal Conference (BAPEC), I was charged with the responsibility of ensuring the integral education of adolescents and youth. I organized catechetical programs for hundreds and thousands of them on various occasions. Most often, these young people were joined together for catechesis or faith education without age distinctions. Reading through the recent *Directory for Catechesis (DC)*, I came across the magisterial recommendation on catechesis according to age groups.⁴ This attracted my attention because of the method I used in the past which pedagogically is wanting as it does

---

[3] Cf. *Catechism of the Catholic Church*, Libreria Editrice Vaticana, Vatican City 1992, n. 5.
[4] Cf. PONTIFICAL COUNCIL FOR PROMOTING NEW EVANGELIZATION, *Directory for Catechesis*, 23 March 2020, The Incorporated Catholic Truth Society, London 2020, n. 245. Henceforth, shall be quoted as *DC*.

not follow the principle of graduality. Moreover, taking cognizance of the two main courses of action in youth ministry as recommended by *Christus Vivit (ChV)* that is *outreach* (meaning the way we attract young people to the Lord) and *growth* (the way we help those who have already had that experience to mature in it),[5] I realized that for a better integral faith education of adolescents and youth, it should be based on the principle of graduality, most especially during the period of adolescence because of its delicateness.

Furthermore, in my research program, taking a close examination of faith education of adolescents and youths in some Parishes in Africa, Latin America, the United States of America, and Europe, I came to realize more that adolescents and youths everywhere have the same challenges, preoccupations, and aspirations with a little difference in systems of education, culture, and environment. In some cases, emphasis may be laid on some areas than on others, but in all, there are more similarities in their uniqueness, and as such, they stand in need of guidance. This is the more reason the Church, more than ever before, stresses the pastoral priority of integral care of the young as can be seen in *ChV, DC*, and *Pastoral Guidelines for the Celebration of World Youth Day in Particular Churches* as shall be examined in this book.

It is my conviction, firstly, that an effective adolescents' and youths' integral faith education that takes into consideration the changes in the sociocultural environment and their stages of life will adequately prepare them for a *better* Church and a *better* society. Secondly, the application of the principle of graduality will facilitate the two main objectives of youth catechesis as outlined in *ChV* number 209 and as echoed in the *DC*, which enunciates that every project of formation which combines liturgical, spiritual, doctrinal, and moral formation is to have two main goals. The first is the development of the *kerygma*, which is the foundational experience of

---

[5] Cf. Francis, *Christus Vivit. Post-Synodal Apostolic Exhortation to Young People and to the entire People of God*, Libreria Editrice Vaticana, Vatican City 2019, n. 72–73. Henceforth, shall be quoted as *ChV*.

encounter with God through Christ's death and resurrection. And the second is *growth* in fraternal love, community life, and service.[6]

To arrive at these convictions, therefore, a good understanding of the physical, cognitive, and emotional development of the stages of these young people and other related sciences in this digital age will establish a fertile background for integral faith education to be translated into their world. This work, therefore, seeks to research the principle of graduality in the integral faith education of adolescents and youth taking into consideration related sciences so that they can grow to maturity into the fullness of Christian life and, with the help of the Holy Spirit, come to encounter Christ for the rest of their lives. As the novitiate is important for religious life and the seminary is for the ordained ministry, so is the pastoral care of young people (youth ministry) or the maturation of the integral faith of adolescence and youth for an effective Christian life as well as a better life in society. The emphasis on adolescence is that it is the peak moment in the life of a human person with physical, psychological, and social challenges, as well as strengths that can be nurtured for a fulfilled life.

Structure

The book begins with a foreword, a preface, and an introduction. Chapter 1 brings out the understanding of the group of persons who are the target of this book, that is, adolescents and youths. The second chapter explains the principle of graduality proposed for the integral faith education of adolescents and youths from the pedagogical standpoint, moral theology, the *Directory for Catechesis (DC)*, and its applicability in various areas. The third chapter brings out the understanding of the concept of integral faith education with enlightenment from experts in that field. Chapter 4, based on the understanding of who adolescents and youths are and what is understood by the principle of graduality and integral faith education, brings out a guide on the catechesis of adolescents and youths. Flowing from

---

[6] Cf. *DC*, n. 253.

chapter 4, chapter 5 treats the tasks and prospects of faith education of adolescents and youths as recommended by the Magisterium. Chapter 6 explains the strategy of the Church in ministering to adolescents and youths, especially in the *digital age*. Chapter 7 considers World Youth Day (WYD) a pastoral guide for every youth ministry based on the directives from the *Dicastery for the Laity, Family, and Life*. And finally, chapter 8 snaps to focus on the necessity of creating a suitable environment for adolescents and youths. The book ends with a conclusion and a select bibliography.

—Fr. Gatien Ngah
October 22, 2022
Feast of Pope Saint John Paul II, Rome

CHAPTER 1

UNDERSTANDING ADOLESCENCE AND YOUTH

1.1. Definition

The term *adolescence* comes from the Latin *adolescere*, which means *to mature*. It is a transitional stage of physical and psychological development that generally occurs during the period from puberty to adulthood.[7] Adolescence is usually associated with the teenage years, but its physical, psychological, or cultural expressions may begin earlier and end later. It should be noted that age provides only a rough marker of adolescence, and scholars have not agreed upon a precise definition.[8] Different nations, states, and cultures may have different ages at which an individual is considered mature enough for society to entrust them with certain privileges and responsibilities. From a general and traditional analysis, it includes persons form the ages ten to twenty-one.[9] According to the outline given by the American Academy of Pediatrics, this period is divided into three stages: early

---

[7] Cf. Brittany ALLEN—Helen WATERMAN, "Stages of Adolescence," *American Academy of Pediatrics*, http://www.healthchildren.org, 28th March 2019.
[8] Cf. John COLEMAN, *The Nature of Adolescence*, Routledge New York, 1980, 2.
[9] Cf. COLEMAN, The Nature of Adolescence, 2.

adolescence from ten to thirteen, middle adolescence from fourteen to seventeen, and late adolescence from eighteen to twenty-one.[10]

According to John C. Coleman, adolescence is a challenge and a delight. It is a challenge because there are undoubtedly many difficulties and obstacles to be overcome if adults and teenagers are to get on well with each other. It is a delight because there is a great pleasure to be gained for adults in the idealism and enthusiasm for life apparent in this stage of young people's development.[11] A thorough understanding of adolescence in society depends on information from various perspectives, including psychology, biology, history, sociology, education, and anthropology. Within all of these perspectives, adolescence is viewed as a transitional period between childhood and adulthood, whose cultural purpose is the preparation of children for adult roles.[12] Understanding the concept of adolescent development can be delineated from various perspectives: biologically, as the physical transition marked by the onset of puberty and the termination of physical growth; cognitively, as changes in the ability to think abstractly and multi-dimensionally; or socially, as a period of preparation for adult roles.[13] This, therefore, implies that the study of adolescent development often involves interdisciplinary collaborations. For instance, in neuroscience or biobehavioral health, the focus can be on pubertal changes in brain structure and their effects on cognition or social relations. For a sociologist, the interest in adolescence studies will be on the acquisition of social roles and how this varies across cultures or social conditions. For a developmental psychologist, the focus might be on changes in relations with parents and peers as a function of school structure and pubertal status. All these areas constitute a package of the world of adolescence, and its understanding will enable an effective integral faith formation for them. In the light of the principle of graduality then, adolescents progress

---

[10] Cf. ALLEN—WATERMAN, "Stages of Adolescence."
[11] Cf. COLEMAN, The Nature of Adolescence, 2.
[12] Cf. Saul MCLEOD, "Erik Erikson Psychosocial Stages," *Simply Psychology*, https://www. Simple psychology.org/Erik-Erikson.html, 3rd May 2018.
[13] Cf. MCLEOD, "Erik Erikson Psychosocial Stages."

biologically, cognitively, psychologically, and sociologically in a gradual manner, and in addition, each child is unique and matters as well. Hence, an examination of the stages of adolescence following the principle of graduality (which shall be dwelled more subsequently in the progress of the work) will contribute to good comprehension. The principle of graduality is applicable in the growth process of adolescents because the physical, cognitive, and emotional aspects do not just all develop automatically and completely. It is the understanding of these stages that enables any catechist or youth minister to translate catechesis into these stages to ensure its fruitfulness. It should be noted that when a child is in his adolescent years, he or she is transitioning both physically and mentally from being a child to an adult. During this period, there are several different stages of development that children must go through. These stages range from early to late adolescence. In each stage, the physical, cognitive, and emotional development shall be examined.

1.2. Stages of Adolescence

1.2.1. Early Adolescence: Ages 10 to 13

Early adolescence is the stage in human growth and development that occurs between the ages of ten and thirteen and is usually associated with the onset of puberty. It is characterized by physical, emotional, and personality changes. This stage is considered the beginning of the period of maturation.[14]

1.2.1.1. Physical Development

At this period of early adolescence, preteens experience both physical growth and sexual development, which can be uncomfortable, and it begins puberty. Puberty comes from the Latin *pubertas* meaning the *age of manhood*. It is the time in life when a boy or

---

[14] Cf. COLEMAN, The Nature of Adolescence, 25.

girl becomes sexually mature.[15] It is a process that usually happens between the ages of ten and fourteen for girls and twelve and sixteen for boys. It causes physical changes and affects boys and girls differently. In girls, the first sign of puberty is usually breast development, and then hair grows in the pubic area and armpits, and menstruation (or a period) usually happens last. In boys, puberty usually begins with the testicles and penis getting bigger, then hair grows in the pubic area and armpits, muscles grow, the voice deepens, and facial hair develops as puberty continues. Both boys and girls may get a skin condition. They also usually have a growth spurt. This term is usually taken to refer to a rapid increase in height and weight that occurs during early adolescence and lasts for about two or three years.[16] This brings them closer to their adult height, which they reach after puberty.[17]

1.2.1.2. Cognitive and Emotional Development

Early adolescents begin to assert more independence as they move through the stages of adolescence.[18] This means they may rebel, especially when parents reinforce rules and set limits. In this age group, there is an increased need for privacy, which is another sign of wanting more independence and less supervision.[19] They may also require more privacy to deal with the curiosity and anxiety that come with body changes and new feelings. In this phase, they may notice or start to question their gender identity. This is something that may continue throughout or even beyond the stages of adolescence. It is common for preteens to become more focused on themselves or a bit egocentric. Their thoughts and feelings are centered on themselves, making them self-conscious. At this point, they start

---

[15] Cf. COLEMAN, The Nature of Adolescence, 25.
[16] Cf. COLEMAN, The Nature of Adolescence, 27.
[17] Cf. NATIONAL INSTITUTE of CHILD HEALTH and HUMAN DEVELOPMENT, "Puberty," *Midline Plus, https://medlineplus.gov/rss.html,* 27th December 2016.
[18] Cf. ALLEN—WATERMAN, "Stages of Adolescence."
[19] Cf. MCLEOD, "Erik Erikson Psychosocial Stages."

feeling like they are always being judged by people, especially their peers. It is also noticed that at this point, early adolescents have a very "black-and-white" thought process—that is, something is either right or wrong—with no room for other interpretations. They see things as either amazing or awful, rarely ever just *okay*.[20]

1.2.2. Middle Adolescence: Ages 14 to 17

Middle adolescence is the second stage of adolescence, which occurs between the ages of fourteen and seventeen. It is a period of significant emotional, intellectual, and social development. Like in early adolescence, physical, cognitive, and emotional development can be identified.

1.2.2.1. Physical Development

Changes from puberty are still happening during middle adolescence. Physical changes in females may have slowed down or finished, but by this age, most will start having regular menstrual periods. Most males will have started their pubescent growth spurt, and their voices begin to lower, and there may be a period where the voice cracks. Acne develops in both males and females.

1.2.2.2. Cognitive and Emotional Development

As the brain continues to develop, thought processes mature. However, they still do not process things like adults yet. The frontal lobes are the last parts of the brain to develop and are not fully mature by this stage. The frontal lobes are responsible for complex decision-making, judgment, impulse control, and considering the consequences of actions.[21] Teens at this age may be able to start thinking in the abstract and start seeing the bigger picture rather than the

---

[20] Cf. ALLEN—WATERMAN, "Stages of Adolescence."
[21] Cf. ALLEN—WATERMAN, "Stages of Adolescence."

specifics of one situation. Abstractness is viewed as a gradual growing process from birth to adulthood.[22] According to Fischer in his skill theory of the development of abstractions, they are first isolated structurations of previously constructed representations. Afterward, abstractions may gradually be organized through mapping and correspondences between previously isolated abstractions, up to more general systems made of several abstractions that are linked together.[23] They can use logic but are still primarily driven by emotion. It is at this stage that most middle adolescents start feeling interested in romantic and sexual relationships. Exploration of their sense of identity, as well as beliefs and values, is common. Some want to fit in with their peers while others want to assert their individuality.[24]

1.2.3. Late Adolescence: Ages 18 to 21

Late adolescence is the last stage in the development of adolescence. It occurs between the ages of eighteen and twenty-one and is a moment of settlement of all the changes experienced throughout this vital period.[25] Little by little, the adolescent recovers the balance lost with the onset of puberty, the result of the acceptance, and integration of all the physical, emotional, and psychological changes experienced. This recovery of balance is necessary to start the transition to adult life in a state of healthy at all levels.

1.2.3.1. Physical Development

The physical changes produced in adolescence are much more intense during the first stage. In late adolescence, there is a progressive deceleration of growth. In this way, hormonal secretions, growth and body changes (such as height, weight, bone mass), and the devel-

---

[22] Sandy JACKSON—Luc GOOSSENS (edd), *Handbook of Adolescent Development* Psychology Press, New York 2019, 77.
[23] JACKSON—GOOSSENS (edd), *Handbook of Adolescent Development*, 77.
[24] Cf. ALLEN—WATERMAN, "Stages of Adolescence."
[25] Cf. ALLEN—WATERMAN, "Stages of Adolescence."

opment of organs and systems (such as sexual maturation, growth of different organs), together with other areas, come to a stop of their progression because of the maturity reached.

1.2.3.2. Cognitive and Emotional Development

The brain is completing its development during late adolescence. However, the frontal lobe will not fully develop until around age twenty-five. That is why some people consider late adolescence to be from ages eighteen to twenty-four.[26] Young people in this age range usually have better impulse control and decision-making skills than those in middle adolescence. Risks and rewards are more accurately evaluated. There is a stronger sense of identity in older adolescents. Values and beliefs are often solidified during this stage. Independence increases as many young adults separate from their parents to live outside their childhood homes. Established relationships with parents, siblings, and other family members may change in nature now that adulthood has nearly been reached.[27]

At this stage, social awareness ends, and a lot of time begins to be spent thinking about situations and processes that are not limited to what can be seen, heard, and touched in the immediate environment. It is a renunciation of the egocentricity typical of the previous stages, although it does not disappear completely. Long-term plans come to occupy a much more important role than before, and the image that is given, although it is still relevant, begins to cease to be one of the main pillars of one's own identity. A good part of the egocentricity that defined childhood and the rest of the adolescent stages is abandoned, making it more likely that these young people are interested in politics and social processes in general since their objectives become more related to what they are beyond their social circles. Thoughts may turn to the future, and decisions may be based on their beliefs, desires, and hopes.[28]

---

[26] Cf. COLEMAN, The Nature of Adolescence, 28.
[27] Cf. COLEMAN, The Nature of Adolescence, 27.
[28] Cf. ALLEN—WATERMAN, "Stages of Adolescence."

The adolescent, during this stage, manages to create a personal identity (the result of the integration of his previous being with his new and free personal choices), creates new social relationships, and internalizes moral and ethical values that will determine his progressive entry and functioning in the adult world. Thought reaches the level of formal operations, which allows it to carry out a series of cognitive operations with which it will evolve in this last stage of adolescent development.

In conclusion to our examination of adolescence and especially in this final stage, following the principle of graduality, therefore, the period of adolescence in general as mentioned before is a gradual and step-by-step transitional period to adulthood. This transition involves the body, mind, and emotions of adolescents and, at the same time, the society in which they live contributes to their growth process.

From these stages of adolescence, as seen above, one can understand that the physical, cognitive, and emotional aspects of these three stages are not the same. Therefore, pedagogically, it will be unwise to apply the same catechetical consideration for all stages in the same respect.

1.3. Youth

It should be recalled that the period of adolescence is a transition to adulthood with its last stage being *late adolescence*. This leads to the next stage, which is *youth* (and in specific terms, the people at this stage are referred to as *young people*). The characteristics of this last stage begin the emotional and psychological thought pattern of settling down given that the basic physical development has been completed. It should be borne in mind that *youth* and *adolescence* are both terms that refer to the early stages of an individual's life. Because of the similarity and the close relation of these two terms, adolescence and youth (young people) often tend to be used interchangeably, and at times, it is acceptable to do so. But following the principle of graduality, it is recommended to make the distinctions, most especially as faith education is concerned. However, by definition, adolescence and youth convey different connotations because of which the two terms must be carefully examined prior to employing them in relation to certain contexts.

Youth is a general term used to convey the early stages of an individual's life. It is often used to refer to young persons who have not yet reached adulthood. However, the most widely accepted belief is that youth refers to the time between childhood and adulthood while the term itself can also be used to imply the characteristics of a young person such as the appearance of freshness, enthusiasm, smartness, and vigor. According to the provisions of the agencies of the United Nations, determining exactly the year span that occurs in youth, this period is placed between fifteen and twenty-five years, thus being one of the most important stages of life to intrinsically define the person, their interests, their projects, and their relationship to the world and everything around it. However, age-based definitions have not been known to be consistent over the years, and as a result, youth has come to mean a general term to refer to a daring, fresh, and energetic mindset and an exuberant physicality.

On the other hand, still in the general sense as previously mentioned, *adolescence* is a term used to refer to the stage of *growing up*, which spans between puberty and legal adulthood—a transitional stage of physiological and physical development and is closely associated with teenage years. Adolescence is normally associated with attributes of growing up such as raging hormones; pubertal and biological changes; changes in height, weight, and muscle mass; and changes in brain structure. However, adolescence in society depends upon various factors such as sociology, biology, history, psychology, and anthropology.

From the explanation above, the terms *youth* and *young people* can be used in a general sense and very often interchangeably with adolescence from the point of view of *growing up*, but at the same time, it is also used in a specific sense. Based on the principle of graduality and the recommendation of the Magisterium that catechesis should be organized according to age groups,[29] there is a strong need for this distinction to be made regarding adolescence and youth.

---

[29] *ChV*, 245.

The period of youth, therefore, follows that of late adolescence, which is between the ages of twenty-two and twenty-nine. According to the age group specified for young people by the Synod of Bishops in the preparatory document for the XV Ordinary General Assembly on the theme, *Young People, the Faith and Vocational Discernment*, young people were placed between sixteen and twenty-nine.[30] In the new *DC* 2020, following the principle of graduality, this age group-range now includes part of middle adolescents (fourteen to seventeen), late adolescents (eighteen to twenty-one), and youth (twenty-two to twenty-nine). The division can continue following the various stages or age groups of human development with young adulthood (thirty to thirty-nine), middle adulthood (forty to sixty), late adulthood (sixty-one to seventy), and aging (seventy-one and beyond). As mentioned already, age-based definitions always vary according to different systems and cultures based on the emphasis, but still, it is recommended to follow a pattern based on the principle of graduality.

This growth process of adolescents and youths is normal and conventional, but in some regions, because of some challenges (be it cultural, economical, social, and the like), they may be forced to grow the hard way and with irregular patterns.

---

[30] SYNOD OF BISHOPS, XV Ordinary General Assembly, "Preparatory Document," on *Young People, the Faith and Vocational Discernment*, Vatican City 2017.

CHAPTER 2

UNDERSTANDING THE PRINCIPLE OF GRADUALITY

2.1. Definition

The principle of graduality or gradualness is a methodology that obtains in Catholic moral and pastoral theology, in psychological developmental theories, and in linguistics and didactic developments. This section shall specifically examine the principle of graduality in moral theology, in pedagogy, in line with the three domains of learning, and in the *DC*.

2.2. The Principle of Graduality in Moral Theology

In Catholic moral and pastoral theology, the principle of graduality holds that "people should be encouraged to grow closer to God and his plan for our lives in a step-by-step manner rather than expecting to jump from an initial conversion to perfection in a single step."[31] Human experience testifies that we are not made perfect upon our initial conversion. We must grow in various ways over time, and we

---

[31] Jimmy AKIN, *The Law of Gradualness* in Catholic Answers Magazine, *https:// www. Principle of gradualness,* 13th October 2014.

must continue to struggle against sin. This principle is evident in the scriptures. Saint Paul says, "I, brethren, could not address you as spiritual men, but as men of the flesh, as babes in Christ. I fed you with milk, not solid food; for you were not ready for it; and even yet you are not ready, for you are still of the flesh" (1 Corinthians 3:1–3).[32]

In the realm of morality, the principle of graduality seems to have come to the fore of the moral theological lexicon particularly when Pope Saint John Paul II referred to it in *Familiaris Consortio (FC)* when he says:

> And so what is known as "the law of gradualness" or step-by-step advance cannot be identified with "gradualness of the law," as if there were different degrees or forms of precept in God's law for different individuals and situations. In God's plan, all husbands and wives are called in marriage to holiness, and this lofty vocation is fulfilled to the extent that the human person is able to respond to God's command with serene confidence in God's grace and in his or her own will.[33]

Though not offering a precise formulation of the principle of graduality, Pope Saint John Paul II, in the same exhortation, points to the proper Christian context which forms the framework in which the principle of graduality or the law of gradualness is to be properly understood:

> What is needed is a continuous, permanent conversion which, while requiring an interior

---

[32] All quotations from the Bible are taken from the New Jerusalem Bible edited by Henry Wansbrough and published by Darton, Longman and Todd Ltd, 1st March 1994.

[33] JOHN PAUL II, *Familiaris Consortio. Apostolic Exhortation on the Role of Christian Family in the Modern World* Libreria Editrice Vaticana, Vatican City 1981, n. 34. Henceforth, shall be quoted as *FC*.

> detachment from every evil and an adherence to good in its fullness, is brought about concretely in steps which lead us ever forward. Thus a dynamic process develops, one which advances gradually with the progressive integration of the gifts of God and the demands of His definitive and absolute love in the entire personal and social life of man. Therefore an educational growth process is necessary, in order that individual believers, families[,] and peoples, even civilization itself, by beginning from what they have already received of the mystery of Christ, may patiently be led forward, arriving at a richer understanding and a fuller integration of this mystery in their lives.[34]

From this quotation, it can be clearly seen that the principle of graduality, properly understood, has its origin in the very reality of human psychomoral development; as in most areas of human development, so too in the moral sphere, maturity manifests itself through a gradual or step-by-step process toward an ever-deeper appropriation of right moral behavior as can be seen in concrete choices and actions. In the Christian context, it articulates the gradual nature of conversion. Genuine conversion places us necessarily on a course that intends steady progress, notwithstanding human weakness and occasional moral failures, toward an ever more consistent and holistic embrace of the truth of Christ's moral teaching.

Historically, as a *law* or *moral principle*, it was applied in the Church's missionary endeavor as a measure for pastorally guiding converts to a steady embrace of moral precepts as presented by the Church.[35] This is the necessary context in which the Church understands the principle of graduality or the law of gradualness. But it is vitally important to understand, as noted in *FC*, that the principle

---

[34] *FC*, n. 9.
[35] Cf. AKIN, *The Law of Gradualness* in Catholic Answers Magazine.

of graduality does not imply that either the convert or the Church should craft and validate individualized and autonomous moral norms as if there were different degrees or forms of precept in God's law for different individuals and situations. That would constitute the very perversion of the law of graduality to which Pope Saint John Paul II refers—namely, *the graduality of the law*. Converts to the faith are to be led and assisted in appropriating the new moral requirements of life in Christ in progressive steps of gradual conversion and exigency; assuring them of God's mercy, presence, and grace; safeguarding against their discouragement; and accompanying them in a step-by-step renewal of life but without diminishing the full import of the moral requirements.

2.3. The Principle of Graduality in Pedagogy

In the psychological, linguistic, and didactic realms, the methodological principle of graduality has its origin in Vygotsky's psychological theory (learning can lead to development) and in the linguistic phenomenon of graduality present at every language level.[36] The term *graduality* has been specified in the theory of speech development by Elena Arkhipova as a progression from the zone of actual speech development to that of a proximal one under the guidance of teaching, which eventually provides the condition for all the elements of the didactical system to manifest themselves with ever-increasing intensity.[37] Graduality in language teaching and speech development methodologies presupposes the partition of the system into several sections, each with a set of means, methods, forms, and techniques of the same kind, devised for different stages of language teaching, with a gradual increase in the content volume and a growing complexity of the methods and forms of its presentation depending on the

---

[36] Cf. Elena ARKHIPOVA, "The Graduality Principle in Language Teaching," *The Linguistic and Didactic Aspects, Future Accademy, https://www.Future Academy.org.UK*, 2nd February 2019.

[37] Cf. ARKHIPOVA, *Theory and practice of teaching the Russian language*, Routledge, Moscow City 2009, 45.

stage and the students' level of speech development. Graduality as a cognitive phenomenon represents an interdisciplinary category of linguistics and linguodidactics. This principle allows us to specify the minimum content to be studied; determine the correlation of methods, forms, and means at every stage of the process of teaching; and develop a system of exercises that become the theoretical basis for language learning progress. It is necessary for the creation of a system of exercises with gradual complication and gradation of speech tasks. In general, it represents the theoretical basis on which the developing system of teaching native language and speech is built, as it marks the milestones for personal, meta-subject, and subject results.

After examining the principle of graduality from the Christian context in the moral theological and pedagogical realms, what is its relation to the three domains of learning, namely cognitive, affective, and behavioral? Its understanding will demonstrate and corroborate the gradual process of adolescents in their integral education.

2.3.1. The Three Domains of Learning

The three domains of learning, also called Bloom's taxonomy, are a set of three hierarchical models used to classify educational learning objectives into levels of complexity and specificity. The models organize learning objectives into three different domains: cognitive (thinking), affective (emotions or feeling), and behavioral (physical or kinesthetic) to be achieved.[38] It is imperative to understand that there are different categories of learners who have varying needs, and as such, different methods must be adopted in the planning and delivery of lessons to ensure that such needs are addressed. These domains have two targets in the pedagogical field. It consists of the part of the teacher or educator and that of the student or learner. On the part of the teacher, it helps to set, organize, and clarify objectives (learning goals) to plan and deliver appropriate instructions, design

---

[38] Cf. Joanne WENGROFF, "What is Bloom's Taxonomy?" *Synapse*, *https://getsynapse.com/blog/what-is-blooms-taxonomy/* 23rd January 2020.

valid assessment tasks and strategies, and ensure that instruction and assessment are aligned with the objectives. On the part of the students, it shows how human beings understand or grasp the knowledge presented by the teacher. This pedagogical interchange between the teacher and student bears testimony to the principle of graduality in that the presentation of knowledge takes a gradual and systematic process as well as the acquisition of that knowledge. It adopts the strategy *"Every child matters"* structure that requires that all learners with different needs are taken into consideration.[39]

According to educational neuroscience consultant David A. Sousa, the three domains of learning, initially developed between 1956 and 1972, have received considerable contributions from researchers and experts in the field of education.[40] Studies by Benjamin Bloom on cognitive domain (1956), David Krathwohl on affective domain (1964), and Anita Harrow on psychomotor domain or behavioral domain (1972) have been encompassed into the three domains of learning.[41] Learning is not an event. It is a gradual process. It is the continual growth and change in the brain's architecture that results from the many ways we take in information, process it, connect it, catalog it, and use it (and sometimes get rid of it).[42] Learning can generally be categorized into three domains as mentioned already, and within each domain are multiple levels of learning that progress from more basic, surface-level learning to more complex, deeper-level learning following the principle of graduality. It is interesting to note that while the cognitive taxonomy was described in 1956 and the affective in 1964, the psychomotor domain was not fully described until the 1970s.

---

[39] Cf. WENGROFF, "What is Bloom's Taxonomy?"
[40] Cf. David SOUSA, *How the Brain Works*, Corwin Press, California 2016, 305.
[41] Cf. SOUSA, *How the Brain Works*, 305.
[42] Cf. WENGER, *Communities of practice. Learning, Meaning, and Identity*, Cambridge University Press, United Kingdom 1998, 202.

2.3.1.1. Cognitive Domain

The cognitive domain contains learning skills predominantly related to mental (thinking) processes. Learning processes in the cognitive domain include a hierarchy of skills involving processing information, constructing understanding, applying knowledge, solving problems, and conducting research.[43] There are six levels of cognitive complexity: knowledge, comprehension, application, analysis, synthesis, and evaluation. It should be noted here that Bloom's taxonomy focused on describing levels of attainments rather than process skills and did not substantially address how the learner proceeds from one level to the next.[44] The cognitive domain includes skill clusters that organize a complete, concise, and complementary listing of the learning skills most critical for each process. The newer version of Bloom's taxonomy of learning has a number of added features that came up in 2001. It includes remember, understand, apply, analyze, evaluate, and create.[45]

The cognitive domain involves the development of our mental skills and the acquisition of knowledge. The six categories under this domain, as indicated above, include the following: The first is *knowledge*, which is the ability to recall data or information. Example: An early adolescent recites the Creed. The second is *comprehension*, which is the ability to understand the meaning of what is known. Example: A catechist explains the sacrifice of the Mass in his own words. The third is the *application*, the ability to utilize an abstraction or to use knowledge in a new situation. Example: A pastor applies what he learned in a pastoral psychology class when he talks to adolescents in crisis. The fourth is *analysis*, the ability to differentiate facts and opinions. Example: A canonist was able to win over a case after recognizing logical fallacies in the reasoning of the offender. The fifth is *synthesis*, the ability to integrate different elements or concepts to form a sound pattern or structure so that a new meaning can be

---

[43] Cf. WENGROFF, "What is Bloom's Taxonomy?"
[44] Cf. WENGROFF, "What is Bloom's Taxonomy?"
[45] Cf. WENGROFF, "What is Bloom's Taxonomy?"

established. Example: A therapist combines yoga, biofeedback, and support group therapy in creating a care plan for his patient. The final category is *evaluation*, the ability to come up with judgments about the importance of concepts. Example: A businessman selects the most efficient way of selling products.

2.3.1.2. Affective Domain

The affective domain involves our feelings, emotions, and attitudes. Most people think of learning as an intellectual or mental function. However, learning is not just a cognitive (mental) function. You can also learn attitudes, behaviors, and physical skills.[46] This domain includes how we deal with things emotionally, such as feelings, values, appreciation, enthusiasm, motivations, and attitudes. It is categorized into five subdomains, namely receiving, responding, valuing, organizing, and characterizing.[47]

By *receiving*, we are referring to the awareness of feelings and emotions and the ability to utilize selected attention. Example: listening attentively to a friend or listening to an adolescent during a counseling session. The second is *responding*, that is, the active participation of the learner. Example: participating in a group discussion or conversation, giving a presentation, or following directions. The third is *valuing*, the ability to see the worth of something and express it. Valuing is concerned with the worth you attach to a particular object, phenomenon, behavior, or piece of information. This level ranges from simple acceptance to a more complex state of commitment. Simple acceptance may include one's desire for a team to improve its skills while a more complex level of commitment may include taking responsibility for the overall improvement of the team. Examples: proposing a plan to improve team skills, supporting ideas to increase proficiency, or informing leaders of possible issues. It is the ability to see the worth of something and express it.

---

[46] Cf. Mohammad HOQUE, "Three Domains of Learning," *The Journal of EFL Education and Research*, Vol. 2, n. 2, www.edrc-jefler.org., September 2016.

[47] Cf. HOQUE, "Three Domains of Learning."

Example: A labor officer shares his ideas on the increase in the salary of laborers. The fourth is *organization*, the ability to prioritize one value over another and create a unique value system. Example: A teenager spends more time on her studies than with her boyfriend. And finally, the fifth is *characterization*, the ability to internalize values and let them control the person's behavior. Example: A Christian performs a charitable action not to be seen or noticed but because it is his/her duty.

2.3.1.3. Behavioral Domain

The behavioral domain or psychomotor objectives are those specific to discreet physical functions, reflex actions, and interpretive movements. It suffices again to indicate here that while the cognitive taxonomy was described in 1956, and the affective in 1964, the psychomotor domain was not fully described until the 1970s.[48] That which is used here is developed by Elizabeth Simpson.[49] Traditionally, these types of objectives are concerned with the physical encoding of information, with movement or with activities, where the gross and fine muscles are used for expressing or interpreting information or concepts. The psychomotor domain is comprised of utilizing motor skills and coordinating them.[50] The seven categories under this are *perception*, the ability to apply sensory information to motor activity. Example: A cook adjusts the heat of a stove to achieve the right temperature for the dish. *Set*, that is, the readiness to act. Example: An obese person displays motivation in performing a planned exercise. *Guided response*, the ability to imitate a displayed behavior or to utilize trial and error. Example: A person follows the manual in operating a machine. *Mechanism*, the ability to convert learned responses into habitual actions with proficiency and confidence. Example: A newly ordained priest can celebrate Mass using the orientation given in class and the guidelines of the rubrics. *Complex overt response*, the

---

[48] Cf. HOQUE, "Three Domains of Learning."
[49] Cf. WENGROFF, "What is Bloom's Taxonomy?"
[50] Cf. HOQUE, "Three Domains of Learning."

ability to skillfully perform complex patterns of actions. Example: typing a report on a computer without looking at the keyboard. *Adaptation*, the ability to modify learned skills to meet special events. Example: A designer uses plastic bottles to create a dress. *Origination*, creating new movement patterns for a specific situation. Example: A choreographer creates a new dance routine.

Conclusively, therefore, the three categories of education—with their specific features and objectives designed to engage students who learn to solve problems, process information, and build their skills using different perspectives—provide an integral approach to learning. Let us now consider the principle of graduality in the *DC*.

2.4. The Principle of Graduality in the *Directory for Catechesis*

The 2020 *DC* is the third general catechetical directory for the universal Church and the first document of its kind since 1997, written to apply the Catholic Church's principles and directives for catechesis to the unique situations and circumstances of the modern era. One of the principles considered is the principle of graduality. It is looked upon in two ways: the pathways of catechesis and catechesis in the world of young people.

2.4.1. Pathways of Catechesis

Following the methodology of the principle of graduality as seen in the realms of pastoral theology, psychological developmental theories, and linguistics and didactic developments, the Magisterium in the *DC* recognizes the need for this principle in the catechetical journey of the Church.[51] To the Magisterium, it becomes reasonable to offer pathways of catechesis that vary based on the participants' different needs, ages, and states of life. As such, it is indispensable to respect anthropological-developmental and theological-pastoral real-

---

[51] Cf. *DC,* n. 225.

ities, taking into account the educational sciences. This is why it is pedagogically important, in the process of catechesis, to attribute to each stage its own importance and specificity.[52] It is in this realization that the Magisterium makes the recommendation of the principle of graduality in the realm of the young.

2.4.2. Catechesis in the World of Young People

In the continuous effort of integral faith education of the young, the Magisterium recognized the great need for a renewed presentation of the faith to young people in a gradual process, especially in the modern and technological era, which should be reinforced and placed in the larger context of youth pastoral care. This, therefore, is characterized by pastoral and relational dynamics of listening, reciprocity, co-responsibility, and the recognition of youthful self-assertion.[53] Based on this, the methodological principle of graduality is recommended here as the *DC* articulates:

> Even if there are no clear boundaries and the approaches typical of each culture play a decisive role, it is useful to divide the time of youth into pre-adolescence, adolescence, youth and young adulthood. It is crucial to develop the study of the world of young people, incorporating the contributions of scientific research and taking into account the situations in different countries.[54]

The principle of graduality comes into play with the recognition of the fact that human development is a step-by-step process, hence the necessity of the division of the time of youth into preadolescence, adolescence, youth, and young adulthood. This will enable an

---

[52] Cf. *DC*, n. 225.
[53] Cf. *DC*, n. 245.
[54] *DC*, n. 245.

effective catechesis when each stage of the gradual growth of young people is taken into consideration. For this paper, we have chosen to study the principle of graduality in the integral faith education of adolescents. That is why, at the beginning of the work, the period of adolescence was divided into early adolescence, middle adolescence, and late adolescence in light of the *DC* (n. 245) as quoted above. This division, therefore, is of help to the catechist or youth minister knowing the characteristics of each gradual stage and employing the method of catechesis necessary and commensurate to that age.

CHAPTER 3

UNDERSTANDING INTEGRAL FAITH EDUCATION

For a better understanding of the concept of *integral faith education*, this work considers two areas of importance. The first area deals with the integral dimensions of faith education, and the second area deals with the perspectives of integral faith education.

3.1. Integral Dimensions of Faith Education

By integral faith education, we are referring to the four main areas of Christian living: spiritual life, human development, knowledge of the faith (intellectual), and apostolic activity, most especially for adolescents and youth.[55] These areas are like the four wheels of a car: If one of them is flat, the whole vehicle has to crawl along. Therefore, integral faith education is geared at getting all the various aspects of life in the catechetical process. The end point of integral faith education for the young is about leading them to Christ and making them be like him to become his faithful and fruitful disciples in the world. The four dimensions are briefly outlined below:

---

[55] Cf. Thomas GROOME, *Christian Religious Education. Sharing Our Story and Vision*, Jossey-Bass Inc., California 1999, 73–77.

3.1.1. Spiritual Dimension

The spiritual dimension or education consists in learning how to develop a friendship with Jesus Christ, which is the heart of Christian life. This friendship is established at Baptism; lived out through the virtues of faith, hope, and love; and nourished by prayer and the sacraments. Just as the heart pumps lifeblood into every part of our body, friendship with Christ infuses meaning and zest into every sector of one's life. Spiritual education of adolescents like all Christians helps in developing this friendship that constitutes our spiritual life. It involves understanding the Christian virtues, the Church's sacramental economy, the different methods of prayer, and the role of Mary and the saints. This dimension has been termed the soul of the formation of every Christian.[56]

3.1.2. Human Dimension

Just as our bones give stability and structure to our bodies, basic human maturity gives solidity to our spiritual life. It is often said that *grace builds on nature; it does not substitute it*. The human dimension or education of adolescents involves growth in the basic virtues common to every mature human person, not only Christians: honesty, self-discipline, responsibility, perseverance, kindness, good manners, loyalty, solidarity, and many others. A lack of this basic human formation is often at the root of slow or stunted spiritual growth and apostolic sterility.[57] That is why the psychological and human development of the various age groups of young people is important, as elaborated in that of the adolescents previously in their gradual stages of growth. As mentioned already with the spiritual education of adolescents as the soul of their Christian formation, the human dimension is the base on which education is built.

---

[56] Cf. Emilio ALBERICH—Jerome VALLABARAJ, *Communicating a Faith that Transforms. A Handbook of Fundamental Catechetics*, KristuJyoti Publications, Bangalore 2004, 128.
[57] Cf. ALBERICH—VALLABARAJ, *Communicating a Faith that Transforms*, 128–129.

3.1.3. Intellectual Dimension

The intellectual dimension brings to focus the saying, "You cannot love what you do not know." Based on the analogy that *if we do not know Christ, we cannot love him, and if we do not know the liberating truth of the Church's teaching, we cannot follow and spread it*, therefore, it becomes compelling in the faith education of adolescents to help them understand the *kerygma*. This dimension answers one of the main objectives of youth catechesis, which is the development of the *kerygma*, which is the foundational experience of encounter with God through Christ's death and resurrection.[58] This, therefore, means that the better adolescents know Christ and his teaching, however, the deeper their Christian convictions will be; and the deeper their convictions are, the more joyful their lives will be. In this light, therefore, intellectual faith education of adolescents according to their stages becomes indispensable because Church doctrine does not exist in a vacuum. It needs to be applied to current issues, made intelligible and attractive for different kinds of people, and enriched by human experience and reflection as they mature in their faith.[59] The *General Catechetical Directory* (*GCD*) cautions that the intellectual building up of the faith of adolescents must by no means be considered merely a kind of addition, but rather, it should be counted as an essential need for the life of faith. The manner of teaching is of special importance. The catechist, in dialogue with the adolescent, must stimulate the mind of the adolescent.[60]

According to Thomas Groome, the pedagogical purpose of the intellectual dimension of faith education is more than just *knowledge* of the faith or the *kerygma*. This is because it should enable people (adolescents in this case) to know it well, to take it to heart and life, to come to personal conviction of its truth claims, and to thus be

---

[58] Cf. *DC*, n. 253.
[59] Cf. Thomas GROOME, *Christian Religious Education*, 115–116.
[60] Cf. CONGREGATION FOR THE CLERGY, *The General Catechetical Directory*, Libreria Editrice Vaticana, Vatican City, 1971, n. 88. Henceforth, shall be quoted as *GCD*.

a little likely to live it so that it becomes something that enhances them personally and morally.[61] The intellectual dimension—like the spiritual dimension, which is the *soul*, and like the human dimension, which is the *base*—is the *means*. This leads us to the apostolic dimension of faith education.

3.1.4. Apostolic Dimension

The apostolic dimension of faith education is based on the fact that adolescents like other young people and Christians are called to be apostles to their peers and the entire world. Pope Francis supports this when he says, "Filled with the love of Christ, young people are called to be witnesses of the Gospel wherever they find themselves by the way they live."[62] He continues to say, like Saint Alberto Hurtado, that being an apostle does not mean wearing a lapel pin; it is not about speaking about the truth but living it, embodying it, and being transformed in Christ. Being an apostle does not mean carrying a touch in hand, possessing the light, but being that light. The Gospel is a message that becomes a life fully lived.[63] Do not be afraid to go and bring Christ into every area of life, to the fringes of society, even to those who seem farthest away and most indifferent, whether in school or sport or social life, in volunteer service or in the workplace, or in the political life of the society.[64] These admonitions of Pope Francis, as seen above, summarize the apostolic dimension of adolescents. The apostolic dimension—like the previous dimensions such as the spiritual dimension, which is the *soul*; and like the human dimension, which is the *base*; and like the intellectual dimension, which is the *means*—is the goal of the entire faith education.

These four dimensions—taken onboard at every stage in the life of the young, be it preadolescence, adolescence, youth, and young

---

[61] Cf. Thomas GROOME, *Will there be Faith. A New Vision for Educating and Growing Disciples*, Harper One, New York 117.
[62] *ChV*, n. 175.
[63] Cf. *ChV*, n. 175.
[64] Cf. *ChV*, n. 177.

adulthood—will better prepare them for an integral life in the Church and in society. For young people, as declared by the Magisterium, after the synod on *Young People, the Faith, and Vocational Discernment* is the "now of God," and it holds the future.[65]

3.2. Perspectives of Integral Faith Education

Thomas Groome brings out clearly three perspectives of Christian faith that make it integral. To him, the pedagogical purpose of Christian religious education is a lived Christian faith with three essential and constitutive dimensions; it is a belief conviction, a trusting relationship, and a lived life of agape.[66] These three dimensions find expression in three activities—that is, faith as believing, faith as trusting, and faith as doing. In another expression, the three activities match up in three ways as he calls them: the way of the head, the way of the heart, and the way of the hand.[67] Furthermore, these three activities also correspond to the three domains of learning as previously seen, that is, cognitive, affective, and behavioral. All this put together brings out clearly the pedagogical perspectives of integral faith education suited for adolescents as well as all young people and adults in their maturation process.[68] It squares with the principle of graduality in that the process of integral faith is a gradual process from believing to trusting and to doing, also expressed as from the head to the heart and to the hands. Let us examine each of the three activities.

3.2.1. Faith as Believing

It should be noted that in Western mentality, faith and belief are often taken to be synonymous. For instance, in the liturgy, especially during the profession of the faith, we begin with *I believe in...*

---

[65] Cf. *ChV*, n. 178.
[66] Cf. GROOME, *Christian Religious Education*, 57.
[67] Cf. GROOME, *Will there be Faith*, 111.
[68] Cf. GROOME, *Christian Religious Education*, 77.

This can also be appropriate, to begin with *I commit myself to…* or *I trust in…* Christian faith is more than belief, especially when *believe* is reduced by post-enlightenment mentality to intellectual assent to statements of belief. But while Christian faith is more than belief, there is certainly a belief perspective to it as it finds embodiments in the lives of people. The perspective of the Christian faith, therefore, requires, in part, a firm conviction about the truths proposed as essential beliefs of the Christian faith. Inasmuch as these beliefs are personally appropriated, understood, and accepted by the Christian, there is therefore a cognitive, or what Dulles calls an *intellectualist*, dimension to the Christian faith.[69]

The equation of faith and belief has two understandings, the illuminist understanding championed by Saint Augustine and the intellectualist understanding expanded by Thomas Aquinas. According to the illuminist understanding of faith in the mind of Augustine, faith is an *a priori* divine illumination within a person's soul. The light of faith is first lit by God within a person, and one comes to know and assent to what one knows to be true by the grace of that inner illumination.[70] This grace within acts upon the person's will and, without violating the freedom of the individual, disposes of the will to assent to the truth of what is presented to the intellect. Augustine places the act of believing in a person's will. Augustine's perspective also has a cognitive component to it. That is, believing by the light of God's grace is to lead to the understanding of what is believed. Understanding comes from the power of the intellect guided by revelation and the Church's teaching. On the other hand, the intellectualist understanding or cognitive dimension expanded by Aquinas situates the act of believing in the intellect. This is because the object of that act is *the true*, which pertains properly to the intellect. Consequently, faith, which is the proper principle of that act, must reside in the intellect. Furthermore, Aquinas stroke the middle ground by combining the illuminist understanding of the faith

---

[69] Cf. GROOME, *Christian Religious Education*, 57–58.
[70] Cf. GROOME, *Christian Religious Education*, 58.

and the intellectual assent approach. As quoted by Groome, Aquinas articulates in the following words: "Now the act of believing is an act of the intellect assenting to the divine truth at the command of the will moved by the grace of God."[71]

When we examine the two perspectives of the illuminists and intellectualists in line with the integral faith education of adolescence, which we advocate in this paper, we will realize that neither each of them—considering the purpose of Christian religious faith education to be a lived reality in the world—promote this purpose. This is because the illuminists turn the mind away from the social and economic problems of society. This brings a dichotomy. On the other hand, the scholastics after Augustine further intellectualized faith and increased the dichotomy between one's faith and one's way of living by seeing faith as a virtue of the intellect and charity as a virtue of the will.[72] That is why one can have faith without charity and could believe in the Good News of Christ without responding to it. In this regard, Dulles notes that to see Christian faith only as belief in the sense of rational assent to official doctrines tends to increase the split between faith and daily life.[73] The Second Vatican Council notes as well that "this split between the faith which many profess and their daily lives deserves to be counted among the more serious errors of our age."[74] Christian faith, then, is always a gift of God's grace. It arises from an inner illumination, which disposes a person to believe. By the same grace of God and the power of our own intellect, the disposition to believe finds expression in stated beliefs about which we come to conviction and to which we give our assent.

Following the principle of graduality then, it is clear that the process of integral faith is a progressive step-by-step affair. This leads us to the next activity of faith as trusting after faith as believing.

---

[71] GROOME, *Christian Religious Education*, 58.
[72] Cf. GROOME, *Christian Religious Education*, 58.
[73] Cf. GROOME, *Christian Religious Education*, 58.
[74] SECOND VATICAN COUNCIL, *Gaudium et Spes. Pastoral Constitution on the Church in the Modern World*, Libreria Editrice Vaticana, Vatican City 1965, n. 43.

3.2.2. Faith as Trusting

The term *faith* comes from the Latin *fidere*, which means to *trust*. The very root of this term implies that being in faith is an activity of trusting.[75] From our foregone examination of the believing activity above, which shows that Christian faith points primarily to a cognitive act, the trusting activity is primarily affective. It is the fiducial dimension of being in faith. According to Groome, this fiducial/affective dimension of Christian faith takes the form of a relationship of trust and confidence in a personal God who saves in Jesus Christ. And this trust finds its expression in loyalty, love, and attachment. Because God is faithful, we can commit ourselves with confidence and trust.[76] Faith and trust are practically synonymous as can be seen in the synoptic Gospels. For instance, in the Gospel of Mark, we read that if a person *trusts in God*, then *faith* can move mountains (cf. Mark 11:22–23). This shows a trusting relationship with God that bears fruits.

Placing an emphasis on this activity of faith as trusting bespeaks a truth that must never be overlooked or taken for granted in the integral process of faith education. This is because the entire message of Christ or the call to God's kingdom is an invitation to a relationship of unbounded trust in the faithfulness of God and in the power of God's grace.[77] Moreover, our realization of the power of God and our dependence leads us to trust, awe, wonder, reverence, adoration, gratitude, and petition on our own part. These feelings are expressed in the liturgy and in prayer, be it personal or communal. This shows dialogue in our relationship with God. As the liturgical symbols express and celebrate our trusting relationship with God, they also become sources of increased trust, especially as they are celebrated in a community. To make this trusting activity integral, it must find expression and be embodied in how we live out our day-to-day existence in our Christian journey. After considering faith as

---

[75] Cf. GROOME, *Christian Religious Education*, 61–62.
[76] Cf. GROOME, *Christian Religious Education*, 61.
[77] Cf. GROOME, *Christian Religious Education*, 61.

believing and now faith as trusting, we move on to consider faith as doing from the perspective of integral faith education.

3.2.3. *Faith as Doing*

In our treatment of the dimensions of integral faith education, we mentioned that the apostolic dimension is the goal of faith formation. This apostolic work is done in the community or in society. The fifth and sixth tasks of catechesis point to education for community life and missionary initiative, respectively. These are based on the love of God and the love of neighbors. The faith education of adolescents, therefore, is to prepare them for life in the community. This is because all Christian service is an expression of love and is performed by Christians to build up the kingdom of God on earth. The Church exists to evangelize, that is, "to carry forth the Good News to every sector of the human race so that by its strength it may enter into the hearts of men and renew the human race."[78] Faith as doing fits exactly into this perspective. The aptest example of faith as doing is the classic presentation of Saint James:

> What good is it, my brothers and sisters, if someone claims to have faith but has no deeds? Can such faith save them? Suppose a brother or a sister is without clothes and daily food. If one of you says to them, "Go in peace; keep warm and well-fed," but does nothing about their physical needs, what good is it? In the same way, faith by itself, if it is not accompanied by action, is dead. But someone will say, "You have faith; I have deeds." Show me your faith without deeds, and I will show you my faith by my deeds. You see that a person is considered righteous by what they do and not by faith alone. As the body without

---

[78] *GCD*, n. 46.

the spirit is dead, so faith without deeds is dead.
(James 2:14–18, 24, 26)

Conclusively, integral faith education for a lived Christian faith has at least three essential activities: believing, trusting, and doing. While they can be distinguished for the sake of clarity, they cannot exist alone or have priority over others. Undoubtedly, there are times and circumstances when one perspective will receive more apparent emphasis than the others. And there are individual Christians who, by disposition, tend to take their life stance more within one perspective or another. But as a lived and integral reality, the life of faith of the community and, to some extent, the faith life of every Christian (adolescent) must include all three activities or perspectives. The religious education that takes the Christian faith as its purpose must be designed to intentionally promote this faith from three perspectives, bearing in mind the principle of graduality from one activity to the other.

CHAPTER 4

CATECHESIS OF ADOLESCENTS AND YOUTH

This chapter on the catechesis of adolescents and youth considers two areas of catechesis: the theoretical consideration and the operational consideration. The theoretical aspect dwells on theories and reflections of experts while the operational aspect looks at the application based on the theories and interpretation of the developmental phase of adolescents such as the physical (biological) and cognitive dimensions as presented in the first chapter.

4.1. Theoretical Considerations

The theoretical consideration of catechesis of adolescents and youths considers the psychosocial perspective as well as the application of the principle of graduality in other realms. From these, the catechetical consideration for adolescents and youth shall be drawn out, using the principle of graduality. The pedagogical contention here is to ensure that with a good understanding of the developmental process of adolescents, rightful catechetical content and method be employed at the right and conducive period for effectiveness.

4.1.1. Psychosocial Perspective of Adolescents

Following the principle of graduality, adolescents are divided into early adolescents, middle adolescents, and late adolescents. This is to acknowledge that each stage has characteristics that are progressive in gradual growth. It is worth noting that, unlike the biological and cognitive characteristics that mostly occur at specific times, the psychosocial effects run throughout the adolescence period and beyond.

The early stages of adolescence are characterized by the dynamic of passage from a safe and familiar situation to something new and unexplored. On the one hand, this can bring forth vigor and enthusiasm and, on the other, bring out a sense of confusion and bewilderment. At this stage, the need to measure oneself and experiment with a lot of things in a bid to search for an identity is very high. This is accompanied by a remarkable development of the physical and emotional dimensions as mentioned already.[79]

In the middle and late stages of adolescence, the main characteristic of this period moves to the drive for independence and, at the same time, the fear of beginning to separate from the family context. This drive for independence and fear of separation from the family create a continual *to* and *fro* between bursts of enthusiasm and setbacks. In this regard, the *DC* says, "Adolescents are in motion, in transit and as such are experiencing precisely a tension, first of all within themselves and then with those who surround them but adolescence is not a pathology that we must combat."[80] To better understand the psychosocial development of adolescents to catechize them, Bradford Brown provides an overview of psychosocial development and adolescent risk-taking or the tension that goes within them.[81] He begins with the primary psychosocial tasks adolescents must accomplish. According to him, there are four key tasks: to stand out, to fit in, to measure up, and to hold.[82] First is to stand out, that is, to develop an identity and pursue autonomy. The second is to fit in; by this, he means to find comfortable affiliations and gain

---

[79] Cf. *DC,* n. 246
[80] *DC,* n. 248.
[81] Cf. Bradford Brown, *The Science of Adolescence Risk-Taking. Workshop Report*, National Academies Press Washington, 2011, 48–52.
[82] Cf. Brown, *The Science of Adolescence Risk-Taking*, 49.

acceptance from peers. The third is to measure up, that is, to develop competence and find ways to achieve. And the fourth is to take hold from the point of view of making commitments to particular goals, activities, and beliefs.[83]

Brown identified two ways in which these basic tasks related to the risks that adolescents take. In the first way, many risk behaviors can either foster or impede the successful accomplishment of these tasks. And in the second way, adolescents may turn to risky behaviors to help themselves cope with the failure to succeed in one of these areas.[84]

There is a strong drive for affiliation and acceptance at this stage. This makes adolescents more open to peer influence and also tends to promote the rapid and hasty development of new relationships without much consideration of the consequences. Risk behaviors are also correlated with several more specific kinds of social situations, including romantic relationships that develop early in adolescence, association with older peers or permissive peer groups, romantic or sexual relationships with older partners, and lax adult supervision. According to Brown, apart from the cognitive and biological processes that affect adolescents' behavior, it is important to understand the meaning that adolescents attach to risky behaviors in the social context in which they encounter them.[85] If teenagers perceive, for example, that having premarital sex with multiple boyfriends or girlfriends, as the case may be, will make them popular and rich, those images may be important to their identity. Within their peer group, they may decide to engage in those behaviors despite awareness of the risks.[86]

The essence of the above background and world of adolescents from a psychosocial point of view helps the catechist and the youth ministers know which doctrinal consideration to take knowing the psychosocial struggle adolescents go through and to be able to under-

---

[83] Cf. BROWN, *The Science of Adolescence Risk-Taking*, 48.
[84] Cf. BROWN, *The Science of Adolescence Risk-Taking*, 49.
[85] Cf. BROWN, *The Science of Adolescence Risk-Taking*, 50.
[86] Cf. BROWN, *The Science of Adolescence Risk-Taking*, 99.

stand their actions rather than judge them with moral standards. The catechist or any youth minister should understand, especially during middle adolescence, when peer pressure is at its peak, that the young person at that moment is going through a lot internally and externally. The effects of this peer pressure on an adolescent in search of his/her identity can be experimentation with attitude and behavior, fear and frustration in trying to toe the line or not, depression, and confusion.[87] This understanding will attract a listening ear and loving accompaniment. A judgmental attitude will scare the young people, thereby defeating the purpose of accompaniment. Furthermore, it should be noted that adolescence is not a pathology that we must combat. It is a normal, natural part of growing up and of the lives of our young people. The Magisterium corroborates this when she admonishes that "it is the concern of the community, chaplains, catechists[,] and youth ministers to make room within themselves for grasping and accepting without judgement and with sincere educational passion this adolescent search for freedom, starting to channel it toward an open and daring life span."[88]

4.1.2. The Application of the Principle of Graduality

The application of the principle of graduality can be seen in the works of some developmental psychologists, cognitive psychologists, and faith educationists. The principle can be referenced in the following works and persons.

James Fowler developed a theory of six stages where he describes how an individual's faith matures as they age gradually.[89] The six stages are *intuitive-projective faith* from the age of two, *mythic-literal faith* when the child starts school, *synthetic-conventional*

---

[87] Josh MCDOWELL—Bob HOSTETLER, *Handbook on Counseling Youth. A Comprehensive Guide for Equipping Youth Workers, Pastors, Teachers, Parents*, World Publishing, Dallas 1996, 145–154.
[88] Cf. *DC*, n. 248.
[89] Cf. James FOWLER, *Stages of Faith. The Psychology of Human Development and the Quest for Meaning*, Harper One, New York 1995, 113.

faith that begins in early adolescence, *individuative-reflective faith* often as a young adult, *conjunctive faith* at midlife and beyond, and finally, *universalizing faith* reached by only a few people in later life.[90] Fowler developed his theory from the works of others who have also made use of the principle of graduality such as Jean Piaget (four stages of cognitive development) and Lawrence Kohlberg (six stages of moral development organized in three levels of preconventional, conventional, and post-conventional), and more so, he was probably influenced by the work of Erik Erikson (eight stages of psychosocial development) and Daniel Levinson (seven stages of seasons of life theory).[91] Fowler argues that it is possible to discern a universal pattern of how a person's faith changes at different stages in their life. He believes there is a correlation between his six stages and the age of the individual.[92]

Jean Piaget's theory of cognitive development suggests that children move through four different stages of learning. His theory focuses not only on understanding how children acquire knowledge but also on understanding the nature of intelligence.[93] Piaget's stages are the *sensorimotor stage*, from birth to two years; the *preoperational stage*, from two years to seven; the *concrete operational stage*, from seven to eleven years; and the *formal operational stage*, from twelve years upward. "Piaget believed that intelligence matures as we develop increasingly effective cognitive structures."[94] John Dacey and John Travers add that we can form cognitive structures because "we[they] have inherited a method of intellectual functioning that enables us[them] to respond to our[their] environment."[95] In Fowler's stages, adolescents are found in stage three of conventional faith, and

---

[90] Cf. FOWLER, *Stages of Faith*, 113.
[91] Cf. FOWLER, *Stages of Faith*, 110.
[92] Cf. FOWLER, *Stages of Faith*, xiii.
[93] Cf. John DACEY—John TRAVERS, *Human Development Across the Lifespan*, McGraw-Hill New York 2006, 40.
[94] DACEY—TRAVERS, *Human Development Across the Lifespan*, 41.
[95] DACEY—TRAVERS, *Human Development Across the Lifespan*, 41.

in Piaget's theory, they can be found in the fourth stage of the formal operational stage from the various ages stipulated.

From the catechetical dimension, **Luciano Meddi** makes reference to the principle of graduality in the Christian initiation process of adolescents.[96] According to him, initiation takes place within a formal process of growth in the faith consisting of four steps: *socialization, evangelization, interiorization,* and *integration*.[97] In the step of socialization, there is a transmission of cultural values, experiences of life, and generation to adolescents. Secondly, evangelization comes in because these adolescents need the message of the Gospel presented to them for salvation. Thirdly, there is an interiorization of the Gospel values that transforms the message into the life of the adolescents so that their consciences are formed in the light of the Gospel and so do their ways of life that flow from it. The fruit of this interiorization is conversion. The final step is the integration of the message, which has become united with the person of the adolescent and makes him/her a disciple in the community and society.[98]

According to Alberich, the principle of graduality is very apt in the pedagogical perspective of catechesis. He attests to this when he intimates that to foster a true process of promotion and maturation in the faith, there is an urgent need to pay attention to graduality in the process of growth.[99]

4.1.3. Catechetical Consideration for Adolescents

Regarding catechesis of the early stage of adolescence, the *DC*, in accordance with the principle of graduality, remarks that in addition to the faith foundation laid by the parents, it is at this level in the faith journey of early adolescents that the image of God received in childhood is redefined. Consequently, three catechetical considerations can be identified; the presentation of the *kerygma*, the for-

---

[96] Luciano MEDDI, *Catechetica*, EDB, Bologna 2022, 231.
[97] MEDDI, *Catechetica*, 231.
[98] MEDDI, *Catechetica*, 231.
[99] Cf. ALBERICH—VALLABARAJ, *Communicating a Faith that Transforms*, 304.

mation of relationships (interpersonal and peer relationships) that are linked to the Gospel, and a question-and-answer session on faith matters. This is articulated thus:

> The presentation of the faith to pre-adolescents (early adolescents) is to take pains to sow within their hearts the seed of the vision of God that can ripen over time: the illustration of the *Kerygma* is to pay special attention to the Lord Jesus as a brother who loves, as a friend who helps one to be at one's best in relationships, does not judge, is faithful, values skills and dreams, bringing one's desires for beauty and goodness to fulfillment. Moreover, Catechesis is urged to recognize the self-assertion of pre-adolescents (early adolescents), to create a context of meaningful group relationships, to create a climate in which questions are welcomed and brought into contact with the presentation of the Gospels.[100]

The above citation on the catechetical proposition for early adolescents takes into consideration the psychosocial development of this stage and its level. Firstly, as mentioned already, the faith received from parents and in the first catechesis is deepened. This squares with the fact that adolescents are very inquisitive to know things including their faith. As such, it is a good time to cater to their doubts and strengthen the foundation of their faith. At this time, their minds are so open to listen and be directed. Also, a concrete type of instruction that would explain the lives and works of the saints and of other outstanding persons, together with reflections on the actual life of the Church, could provide adolescents of this age with wholesome nourishment.

---

[100] *DC*, n. 247.

Secondly, in their search for an identity, they tend to establish relationships with their mates and form groups of peers who are a support system in their growth. These friends have their strengths and weaknesses; the presentation of Jesus Christ as a brother and true friend *par excellance* will go a long way to help them. In this regard, *ChV* attests that friendship is one of life's gifts and grace from God. Through our friends, the Lord refines us and leads us to maturity. Faithful friends, who stand at our side in times of difficulty, are also a reflection of the Lord's love and his gentle and consoling presence in our lives. The experience of friendship teaches us to be open, understanding, and caring toward others; to come out of our own comfortable isolation; and to share our lives with others. For this reason, there is nothing so precious as a faithful friend.[101] Jesus, to show the importance of friendship, refers to himself as a friend. "I do not call you servants any longer, but I call you friends" (John 15:15). Through the gift of his grace, we are elevated in such a way that we truly become his friends. With the same love that Christ pours out on us, we can love him in turn and share his love with others as young people, in the hope that they, too, will take their place in the community of friendship he established. True enough, Jesus, who is our best friend, is in heaven, but on our part, we can work generously to help him build his kingdom in this world by bringing his message, his light, and, above all, his love to others.[102]

Furthermore, the *General Catechetical Directory* (*GCD*) notes that the principal task of catechesis in adolescence will be to further a genuinely Christian understanding of life. It must shed light on the Christian message on the realities, which have a greater impact on the adolescent, such as the meaning of bodily existence, love, and the family; the standards to be followed in life, work, and leisure; and justice and peace.[103]

Moreover, the Magisterium in *DC* proposes the creation of meaningful group relationships for this age group. These groups will

---

[101] Cf. *ChV*, n. 151.
[102] Cf. *ChV*, n. 153.
[103] *DC*, n. 84.

provide an avenue for catechesis to be given to them. In other parts of the world, in Dioceses and Parishes, there are associations with a particular spirituality laid down for young people to follow. For instance, in the ecclesiastical province of Bamenda, Cameroon (Africa), there are groups like Cadets of Mary Immaculate and St. Stephen Guild or Altar Servers for boys and girls. In the Cadets of Mary, there are four stages: Aspirancy, Junior Cadets, Senior Cadets, and Children of Mary. The main aim of the group is to follow Mary in her obedience, faith, and charity. Following the principle of graduality, the first stage is for children, the second for early adolescents, the third for middle adolescents, and the fourth for late adolescents and youth. The St. Stephen Guild is an association for boys and girls who serve at the altar during liturgical celebrations. Following the principle of graduality, these boys and girls are divided into four stages: postulants (children), Junior Acolytes (early adolescents), Senior Acolytes (middle adolescents), and Master of Ceremonies (late adolescents, youths, and young adults). This is the ideal structure of these two groups which are avenues of catechesis, but in practice, most often the main criteria for moving to the next stage is not one's age pedagogically as it should but the ability of the candidate to fulfill the requirements of the group in such fashion that you will find early adolescents as senior cadets or senior acolyte as the case may be. In contrast, if the ideal structure of these groups is respected, it can be a veritable ground for the principle of graduality in catechesis to be translated into the stages of these groups.

Thirdly, given that this stage is that of tension and confusion brought by discoveries in the developmental process in the search for identity and in the experimentation of things good, bad, and indifferent, adolescents have quite a lot of inquiries to make and doubts to be clarified. That is why the Magisterium recommends that pains should be taken to create sessions whereby their questions on faith matters as well as the challenges they face in their growth process can be resolved. This is not the work of one person but that of the entire community as Pope Francis exhorts that the community has an important role in the accompaniment of young people; it should feel collectively responsible for accepting, motivating, encouraging, and challenging them. All should regard young people with understanding, appreciation, and affection and avoid constantly judging them or demanding of them perfection beyond their years.[104]

With adolescents in the middle and late stages, considering the dangers, risks, and tensions that surround them, the Magisterium recommends that these adolescents need to have convinced and compelling witnesses by their side to guide them.[105] In the realm of young persons, and especially this particular difficult youthful stage, one of the challenges of catechesis is precisely that of lack of testimony lived out in the families where these adolescents come from and their social groups. At these stages in the life of adolescents, there is generally a drop in Church attendance and many other values learned in childhood. However, this drop does not mean that the quality of catechesis received in childhood and early adolescence was not properly done, but rather that, at this point, the adolescents need to be attracted by joyful and lively activities. Most adolescents evaluate their chaplains, catechists, adult figures, and older peers on how much they understand them and put their authenticity to a demanding test and, therefore, stand in need of those in whom they can see a faith that is lived out with joy and consistency. The Magisterium, therefore, recommends that it is the concern of the community to identify for the service of catechesis those persons who are best able to relate to their world, illuminating it with the light and joy of faith.[106] This indicates that it is not anybody who can work with young people, especially adolescents. This is an eye-opener for those making appointments in various Dioceses and Parishes to know that it is not enough just to appoint any person to be a chaplain to the young, an animator, or any catechist for the faith education of adolescents. It is therefore important to train youth workers before appointing them to cater to the young and that catechesis be carried out as part of the pastoral care for young people, with a strongly educational and voca-

---

[104] Cf. *ChV*, n. 243.
[105] Cf. *ChV*, n. 249.
[106] Cf. *DC*, 249.

tional connotation, in the context of the Christian community and of the life environment of adolescents.

4.1.4. Catechetical Consideration for Youth

The challenge of integral education is one of the challenges facing young people, especially in Africa. The greater population of Africa is made up of young people who are in most need of integral faith education. In this regard, Pope Saint John Paul II remarked that the Church in Africa knows well that youth are not only the present but above all the future of humanity[107] and made this recommendation:

> It is thus necessary to help young people to overcome the obstacles thwarting their development: illiteracy, idleness, hunger, drugs. In order to meet these challenges, young people themselves should be called upon to become the evangelizers of their peers. No one can do this better than they. The pastoral care of youth must clearly be a part of the overall pastoral plan of Dioceses and Parishes, so that young people will be enabled to discover very early on the value of the gift of self, an essential means for the person to reach maturity. In this regard, the celebration of World Youth Day is a privileged instrument for the pastoral care of youth, which favours their formation through prayer, study[,] and reflection.[108]

This recommendation made by Pope Saint John Paul II is not only limited to the young people of Africa, but he made a similar recommendation to young people in all continents of the world. Three areas are worthy of note: Firstly, young people are the best evan-

---

[107] Cf. *EA*, n. 93.
[108] *EA*, n. 93.

gelizers for themselves, and as such, they should be helped to play this role. Secondly, integral faith education (catechesis) of the young should be the priority of every Diocese and Parish, and thirdly is the importance of WYD in the pastoral ministry of adolescents and youth (as shall be treated in chapter 7). These are areas that constitute the stronghold of catechesis for youth.

Furthermore, youths have hopes and aspirations, and as they grow, they seek to realize their dreams. It is noticeable among young people that rapid cultural and social transformation affects them. *Two areas most renowned in the dreams of young people are the desire to further their education at various levels and gain specialization and the desire to gain employment and satisfy their needs.* To some, when their basic necessities are attained, the rest, including needs for growth, can follow. As a result, many young people feel the need to relocate to areas where they can best achieve their dreams.[109] In areas marked by persistent economic underdevelopment, a lack of jobs, conflicts, and insecurities, a good number of young people can easily experience disappointment and boredom, which, at times, give rise to anguish and depression. As a result, much migration takes place, as can be witnessed in many countries in Africa. Some of them feel a general lack of hope concerning their future and are forced into conditions of life that are often humiliating.[110]

On the other hand, from the point of view of religious experience, a great variety can be noted. Many young people demonstrate a drive toward the search for meaning, solidarity, and social engagement. They are often open to religious practices and sensitive to different spiritualities and Church affairs. They participate actively and with enthusiasm in the life of the Church and in their missionary and service experiences and lead an authentic and intense prayer life as can be seen in most Parishes.[111] Also, many young people, because

---

[109] Cf. *DC*, n. 250.
[110] PONTIFICAL COUNCIL FOR PROMOTING NEW EVANGELIZATION, *Directory for Catechesis*, 23 March 2020, The Incorporated Catholic Truth Society, London 2020, n. 250. Henceforth, shall be quoted as *DC*.
[111] Cf. *DC*, n. 250.

of misplaced priorities and different inclinations, fall away from Church activities or display indifference or distrust toward it. The *DC*[112] brings out some of the causes of this fallback. Some of these are as follows:

- Lack of witness, credibility, and spiritual and moral support on the part of the family
- Inadequate catechesis and a Christian community that is hardly meaningful and encouraging

Faced with these causes and the understanding of the situation of young people as painted above, the question is, What strategy can be employed to pastorally minister to them in these circumstances? Each youth minister or catechist should therefore take into consideration these areas highlighted in catechizing this particular group and devise a strategy that suits (chapter 6 shall consider some of these strategies).

4.1.5. *Youth Culture and Popular Youth Ministry*

Deep down, in every young person is the desire to be together with others, to identify with peers, to seek pleasure in various places of encounter, and to make new friends and new encounters. This is what has been termed *youth culture*. In other words, it refers to the societal norms of children, adolescents, and young adults. Specifically, it comprises the processes and symbolic systems that are shared by the youth and are distinct from those of adults in the community.[113] An emphasis on clothes, popular music, sports, vocabulary, and dating typically sets youth apart from other age groups.

The search for daily pleasure leads young people to the experimentation with new ways of being such as entering into relationships; strolling with peers on the streets, in cinema halls, in clubs

---

[112] Cf. *DC*, n. 250.

[113] Frank FASICK, "Parents, Peers, Youth Culture and Autonomy in Adolescence" in *Semantic Scholar* 1984, n.143–157.

and dancing places, and in sporting grounds; and meeting in various restaurants where they can share a meal with friends and identify with them and many others. More so, young people's desire to be together becomes visible in the areas of music and dancing. This is because it constitutes a meeting place and confluence of different instances such as having fun, a momentary escape from some internal/external challenges faced at home or in society, sharing feelings of love and affection, and many others. This is what Michel Maffesoli, a French sociologist, calls *tribalization of youth culture*. This is in reference to the fact that young people gather together because they share a common interest and lifestyle.

These areas play a leading role in the lives of the young. It is therefore important to create more opportunities for them to meet in the community and use the gatherings to give them integral education for a better future. This is why Pope Francis proposes an approach called *popular youth ministry*. It is a kind of youth ministry that is out of the ordinary well-planned pastoral ministry that Parishes and movements carry out, and it is a youth ministry with a different style, schedule, pace, and method. Broader and more flexible, it goes out to those places where real young people are active as mentioned above, and fosters the natural leadership qualities and the charisms sown by the Holy Spirit. It tries to avoid imposing obstacles, rules, controls, and obligatory structures on these young people in the various meeting places. Each youth minister needs only to accompany and encourage them, trusting a little more in the genius of the Holy Spirit, who acts as he wills.[114]

4.2. Operational Considerations

After understanding the principle of graduality in the integral faith education of adolescents and youth—as well as its relation to the three domains of learning: cognitive, affective, and behavioral, corresponding to the integral perspective of believing, trusting, and

---

[114] *ChV.* n. 230.

doing—and at the same time integral dimensions of the faith education such as spiritual, human, intellectual, and apostolic, we now look specifically at its interpretation in the process of faith education of adolescents and youth.

4.2.1. The Principle of Graduality and Communication of the Faith to Adolescents

The goal of communicating the faith to adolescents is for them to live the fullness of Christian life. And secondly, in accordance with the principle of graduality, therefore, this faith is to be communicated in a gradual step-by-step process, taking into consideration the stages of adolescents and their cognitive capacities. For effective communication of integral faith to adolescents, we shall look at the principle of graduality and communication of the faith to adolescents from two perspectives; some guidelines involved in effective communication of the faith and the language which, adolescents and young people speak, in which catechesis needs to be translated.

4.2.1.1. Guidelines of Effective Faith Communication

First, *the principle of clarity*[115] in ideas should be considered. This implies that each topic taken up for catechesis, say, the sacraments, should be clear in the mind of the catechist as to what he wants to say. In the words of Thomas Groome, the foundational question of *the what*[116] should be asked and answered; in other words, the clarity of the question of content and method is such that the clearer the thought, the more effective the communication of the faith to the adolescent.

Second, given the intellectual capacity of adolescents and taking into consideration their attractions, it is important to take cogni-

---

[115] Cf. HARAPPA DIARIES, "The Principles of Communication," www.harappadiaries.com, 7th May 2021.
[116] Cf. GROOME, Christian Religious Education, 3–4.

zance of the *principle of appropriate language*.[117] According to this principle, communication should always be in a simple language. Ideas should be clear to the group in question and be devoid of any doubt. Technical words and words with various meanings should be used to the minimum. Other areas of communicative languages that appeal to adolescents the most and the entire realm of young people should be made recourse to. In this regard, therefore, Alberich sees a need for a catechesis that is open to a variety of communicative languages such as symbol, testimony, celebration, art, and mediatic communication rather than one that is limited to catechism and purely verbal transmission.[118]

The third is the *principle of attention*.[119] The purpose of communicating the faith to adolescents is such that they should clearly understand its meaning or the catechesis given. It means merely transferring information is not communication, and it is important that the receiver understand it. This is possible only when the receiver takes interest in the message and listens to it attentively. This touches on *the why*, as the second foundational question in Groome's pedagogy of religious education.[120] This is also connected to what Alberich calls a shift from catechesis limited to the transmission of the patrimony of faith to that of the education of internalized attitudes of faith, taking into consideration the three levels of cognition, affection, and behavior.[121]

The fourth is the importance of the *principle of feedback*,[122] which is likened to what the *DC* calls the *human experience*,[123] in this case, the human experience of adolescents. According to this principle of feedback in effective communication, it is essential for the sender of the message to know about the success of the message. It means

---

[117] Cf. HARAPPA DIARIES, "The Principles of Communication."
[118] Cf. ALBERICH—VALLABARAJ, *Communicating a Faith that Transforms*, 304.
[119] Cf. HARAPPA DIARIES, "The Principles of Communication."
[120] Cf. GROOME, Christian Religious Education, 33.
[121] ALBERICH—VALLABARAJ, *Communicating a Faith that Transforms*, 304.
[122] Cf. HARAPPA DIARIES, "The Principles of Communication."
[123] Cf. *DC*, n. 197.

that he should see whether the receiver has understood the message or not. Feedback is easily obtained in face-to-face communication with the help of the receiver's facial reactions. Looking at this step of communicating the faith to adolescents, the *DC* corroborates that the experience of the adolescents or of society be approached with an attitude of love, acceptance, and respect. This is because God acts in every person's life and in history, and the catechist, youth animator, or youth chaplain imitates Jesus by being open to this presence. This sets him free from thinking of the person and of history solely as recipients of the initiative and establishes a relationship of reciprocity and dialogue by listening to what the Holy Spirit is already silently accomplishing.[124]

Finally, considering the changes that take place in the growth process of adolescents and youth, the *principle of flexibility*[125] in effective faith communication is of importance. According to this principle, a communication system should be able to adapt to the changes in the organization, and any communication system that cannot adjust to changes according to the need becomes meaningless. These five principles for effective faith communication to adolescents are of prime importance in their gradual growth process in faith.

4.2.1.2. Guidelines on the Language of Young People

In communicating the faith to adolescents following the principle of graduality, it is important to take into consideration the recommendation of *DC* on the language of adolescents and young people in which their gradual maturation in faith takes place. It stipulates the following:

> One consideration of a general character regards the question of the language of young people. The new generations are, in general, strongly

---

[124] Cf. *DC*, n. 197.
[125] Cf. HARAPPA DIARIES, "The Principles of Communication."

> marked by *social media* and by what is referred to as the virtual world. This offers an opportunity that the previous generation of young people did not have and at the same time it presents dangers. It is of great importance to consider how the experience of relationships mediated by technology may structure the conception of the world, of reality, and of interpersonal relationships. Hence the pressing need for pastoral activity to adapt catechesis for young people by translating the message of Jesus into their language.[126]

In the quote above, two things mark the language of young people (adolescents) in faith communication in this generation, that is, firstly, social media and what is referred to as the virtual world, and secondly, technological advancement. And these two areas are fueled by their strong potential for creativity, enthusiasm, and the desire for change in the world and in the Church. This is what is referred to as the language and world of adolescents. Adolescents in this generation are therefore defined as *digital natives*. Hence, to educate them, one needs to translate any catechetical consideration into their world and their language.

The synod on young people made proposals to renew the young ministry so that it should be able to enter into dialogue with the contemporary youth culture or the world of adolescents and young people and their language. Two main courses of action are stressed: *outreach* and *growth*. *Outreach* refers to the way to attract new young people to an experience of the Lord and *growth* refers to the way to help young people who have already had that experience to mature in it.[127]

In the domain of *outreach*, *ChV* attests to the fact that young people themselves know how best to understand their world and

---

[126] Cf. ALBERICH—VALLABARAJ, *Communicating a Faith that Transforms*, 304.
[127] Cf. *ChV*, n. 209.

language and how to find appealing ways to come together. They know how to organize events, such as sports competitions, and ways to evangelize using social media, through text messages, songs, videos, and other ways. They only have to be encouraged and given the freedom to be motivated about evangelizing other young people wherever they are to be found. This implies that they know how and where to transmit messages to their peers.[128] *ChV* in this light continues to enlighten: "We need to use above all the language of closeness, the language of generous, relational and existential love that touches the heart, impacts life, and awakens hope and desires."[129] This means that young people need to be approached with the grammar of love, not by being preached at. The language that young people understand is spoken by those who radiate life, by those who are there for them and with them, and those who, for all their limitations and weaknesses, try to live their faith with integrity.

In the domain of *growth* and effective maturity in the faith, the Magisterium recommends that we divide young people according to preadolescence, adolescence, youth, and young adulthood, following the principle of graduality, and in our case of consideration, according to early adolescence, middle adolescence, and late adolescence. In the process of the adolescents' maturation of faith, language is very important, just as it is vital in the daily communication of messages to others. Catechesis to adolescents consequently should take note of their different ages, environment, capacity, and culture. In the general catechetical process of the Church, faith is expressed in a language. That is why in her history, she has communicated her faith through sacred Scripture (*biblical language*); liturgical symbols and ceremonies (*symbolic-liturgical language*); the writings of the fathers, creeds, formulations of the Magisterium (*doctrinal language*); and the witness of the saints and martyrs (*performative language*). These, together with ethnic languages for the inculturation of the faith and the new technologies and tools, have ushered in another dimension

---

[128] Cf. *ChV*, n. 210.
[129] *ChV*, n. 211.

of language. It is in this backdrop that the Magisterium realizes that in as much as the main languages of the faith are important, they do not appeal the most to the young. As such, there is a greater need for renewal of the presentation of the faith to them, taking into consideration their environment and new technologies for which they are products.

4.2.1.3. Guidelines from the "Principle of Graduality" in the Adolescence Life of Jesus

It is interesting to note that in God's plan of salvation for mankind, the principle of graduality is respected from the point of view of gradual developmental growth in the life of Jesus, the second person of the Trinity. Jesus did not come to redeem the world as a grown man, but his life bears testimony to a step-by-step growth process. Although after the infancy narrative of Jesus with the last incident portraying him as a tiny refugee in Egypt (cf. Matthew 2:14–15) and repatriation in Nazareth (cf. Matthew 2:19–23), the Gospel tells us nothing about his childhood, it does recount several events of his adolescence and youth. Matthew situates the time of his youth between two events: his family's return to Nazareth after their exile and his Baptism in the Jordan, the beginning of his public ministry. Our first image of Jesus as a young adult shows him standing among the crowds on the banks of the Jordan River to be baptized by his kinsman John the Baptist, just like any other member of his people (cf. Matthew 3:13–17). It is important also to add that he lived his prime life as a young adult and died as a young adult.[130] This is to show that the life of Jesus follows the principle of graduality. Our main concern here is the adolescent life of Jesus.

His early adolescent life can be seen when he returned with his parents to Nazareth after being lost and found in the temple (cf. Luke 2:41–51). There, we interpret some catechetical values from his life to be used for adolescents today; "he was obedient to them"

---

[130] Cf. *ChV*, n. 24.

(Luke 2:51); he did not disown his family. Luke then adds beautifully bringing out the principle of graduality that Jesus "grew in wisdom, age[,] and grace before God and men" (Luke 2:52). In a word, this was a time of preparation when Jesus grew in his relationship with the Father and with others. Pope Saint John Paul II explained that he did not only grow physically, but he there was also a *spiritual growth* in Jesus because the *fullness of grace* in Jesus was in proportion to his age: There was always *a fullness*, but *a fullness* which increased as he grew in age.[131] We can therefore say that the adolescence life of Jesus and consequently that of his youth set him on the path to that sublime mission.

Moreover, another catechetical value for adolescents of today is that Jesus's relationship with the Father was that of the beloved Son. Drawn to the Father, he grew up concerned for his affairs: "Did you not know that I must be about my Father's business?" (Luke 2:49). This statement of Jesus, seen in the light of some of the psychosocial characteristics of adolescents, x-rays the desire for autonomy and independence from the family in pursuit of one's goals and identity. Still, it must not be thought that Jesus was a withdrawn adolescent or a self-absorbed youth. His relationships were those of an adolescent who shared fully in the life of his family and his people. He learned his father's trade and then replaced him as a carpenter. At one point in the Gospel, he is called the "carpenter's son" (Matthew 13:55) and another time simply "the carpenter" (Mark 6:3). This is an indication that he was also like another adolescent or young person in his environment. We are made to understand that no one regarded him as unusual or set apart from others; that is why when he began to preach, people could not imagine where he got this wisdom: "Is this not Joseph's son?" (Luke 4:22).[132]

Unlike adolescents of today and probably those of his time, Jesus did not grow up in a narrow and stifling relationship with his parents, Mary and Joseph, but he readily interacted with the wider

---

[131] Cf. *ChV,* n. 26.
[132] Cf. *ChV,* n. 28.

family, the relatives of his parents, and their friends. Hence, we can understand why, when he returned from his pilgrimage to Jerusalem, his parents readily thought that, as a twelve-year-old boy, he was wandering freely among the crowd, even though they did not see him for an entire day, supposing him to be in a group of other adolescents or peers. This shows that he had a normal and good relationship with his parents, relatives, peers, and others in the community.

These highlighted areas demonstrate the fact that the life of Jesus here on earth followed the principle of graduality, and he remains a perfect example for adolescents to identify with as someone who lived their life and pointed the way to follow—the way and life that he is in himself.

CHAPTER 5

GOALS AND TASKS OF FAITH EDUCATION OF ADOLESCENTS AND YOUTH

5.1. Goals of Faith Education

Tasks and prospects of faith education of adolescents and youth are based on the two main goals of catechesis as outlined in *ChV*. The first is the development of the *kerygma*, which is the foundational experience of encounter with God through Christ's death and resurrection. And the second is the *growth* in fraternal love, community life, and service.[133] These two goals combine liturgical, spiritual, doctrinal, and moral formation. These goals peculiar to the faith education of adolescents and youth are derived from the general goals of catechesis as explained in the new *DC*.

1.1.1. Communion with Jesus Christ

The first and central goal of every process of catechesis is the *living encounter with Jesus Christ*. This, therefore, means that the definitive aim of catechesis as enlightened by Pope Saint John Paul II is "to put people not only in touch but in communion, in intimacy, with

---

[133] Cf. *ChV*, n. 213, *DC*, n. 253.

Jesus Christ: only He can lead us to the love of the Father in the Spirit and make us share in the life of the Holy Trinity."[134] Consequently, communion with Christ is the center of Christian life and the center of catechetical action. The work of every youth minister, teacher, or catechist will be to lead these young people to a living encounter with Jesus Christ.

1.1.2. Integral Formation

The second goal, which flows from the first, is the *integral formation of the entire personality.*[135] This second goal is the basis on which the title of this book is designed: *The Integral Faith Education of Adolescents and Youth*. Every catechetical action in general is to form the mind, the heart, and the actions (senses), as explained before. It should target the head, heart, and hands. Furthermore, it should involve the spiritual, intellectual, human, and pastoral dimensions of the person (child, youth, and adult).

1.1.3. Conversion

The third is the *conversion of the person* or deepening the initial conversion of the Christians[136] and, in this case, adolescents and youth. This is to fulfill the summary of the Gospel of Christ as resounded in Mark 1:15, Luke 4:43, and Matthew 4:17; *repent and believe the Gospel for the kingdom of God is near at hand.*

---

[134] JOHN PAUL II, *Catechesi Tradendae. Apostolic Exhortation on Catechesis Today*, Libreria Editrice Vaticana, Vatican City 1979, n. 5. Hence, shall be quoted as *CT*.
[135] Cf. *DC*, n. 76.
[136] Cf. *DC*, n. 77.

INTEGRAL FAITH EDUCATION OF ADOLESCENTS AND YOUTH

1.1.4. Confession of Faith in the One God

The last goal of catechesis is to lead the Christian to the *confession of faith in the One God: Father, Son, and Holy Spirit.*[137] This goal prepares the young people (Christians) to become witnesses of the Triune God and to carry the mission to the ends of the earth. This, therefore, fulfills the mission *Ad Gentes*: "Go make disciples of all nations, baptize them in the name of the Father, and of the Son and of the Holy Spirit, and I will be with you till the end of time" (Matthew 28:19).

1.2. Tasks of Faith Education

In a bid to realize the goals of faith education as explained above, the catechesis of adolescents and youth like that of the entire Christian body has some tasks recommended by the Magisterium inspired by the pedagogy of Jesus Christ in forming his disciples. He got them to *know* the mysteries of the kingdom, taught them to pray, proposed to them *gospel values,* initiated them into a life of *communion* with him and among themselves, and into *mission* as he sent them out after forming them.[138] The faith needs to be known, celebrated, lived, and turned into prayer. To offer an integral faith education to adolescents and youth, as well as all Christians, the following tasks and prospects need to be the target of every catechesis: promoting knowledge of the faith, initiating the celebration of the mystery, forming for life in Christ, teaching to pray, introducing to community life, and missionary life.

5.2.1. Promoting Knowledge of the Faith

The first task is the promotion and development of the *kerygma.*[139] Saint Paul in the letter to the Romans asks a question: "How

---

[137] Cf. *DC*, n. 78.
[138] Cf. *DC*, n. 79.
[139] Cf. *CT*, n. 25.

can they believe in him of whom they have not heard?" (Romans 10:14). This question points to the fact that adolescents need to be educated first and foremost in the doctrine of the catholic faith according to their level. This will be the maturation of the faith they received during their sacramental catechesis.

5.2.2. Liturgical Education

The second task is that of liturgical faith education.[140] The faith of the Church is professed in the *Creed*, celebrated in the *Sacraments*, lived in the *Commandments*, and prayed in the various payers of the Church such as *Mass, liturgy of the hours*, and others. Living out the faith involves always incorporating the catholic liturgical year. Adolescents should be made to understand, for instance, what the seasons of the Church are and what is required from every Christian during each period, what is Mass, and what is expected from every catholic Christian during Mass. Other areas such as the liturgy of the hours, various devotions, the celebrations of the various sacraments of the Church, and many others form part of liturgical education.

5.2.3. Moral Formation

The third task is that of moral education.[141] We have examined previously the goal of religious faith education, which is a lived Christian faith. This points to the moral life of adolescents and all Christians. The task therefore will be to enable them to live a moral life in accordance with natural law and God's law as taught by the Church. Moral values such as Christian modesty, the inalienable right to life from conception to natural death, the care for the poor and needy, and all aspects of morality can also be taught.

---

[140] Cf. *CT*, n. 23.
[141] Cf. CT, n. 22

INTEGRAL FAITH EDUCATION OF ADOLESCENTS AND YOUTH

5.2.4. Teaching to Pray

Adolescents should be taught the centrality of prayer in their lives by beginning and ending every activity with prayer. They could be taught frequent Mass attendance, the *Divine Office*, the Rosary, meditation, spiritual reading, impromptu prayers throughout the day, the Angelus, or others. The life of a Christian must be permeated by prayer. Any true catechesis must involve prayer in every lesson.

5.2.5. Education for Community Life

This task prepares adolescents to live in communities and participate actively in the life and mission of the Church. The faith must be internalized and lived out as a community. Pope Francis notes in *Evangelii Gaudium* (*EG*) that "even if it is not always easy to approach young people, progress has been made in two areas: the awareness that the entire community is called to evangelize and educate the young, and the urgent need for the young to exercise greater leadership."[142] Adolescents should, therefore, be educated to be involved in Parishes not only for devotions and Mass but also for helping others who are in need. Education for community life suggests that adolescents be prepared to take the love they have received from God and share it within the community and to take on the attitudes of Jesus. This calls for them to have an attitude of service, a spirit of simplicity and humility, and concern for the poor and alienated. They should be educated to correct gently, pray, learn forgiveness, and welcome and show love to others. This is particularly important because adolescents are apostles to themselves among their peers, and they can be the first image of Christ they encounter when they brave their way to the Church. Another aspect of this task calls for ecumenical awareness. Having a basic knowledge of other Christian traditions is important for adolescents. These young persons in some of

---

[142] FRANCIS, *Evangelii Gaudium. Apostolic Exhortation on the Proclamation of the Gospel in Today's World*, Libreria Editrice Vaticana Vatican City, 2013, n. 106. Henceforth, shall be quoted as *EG*.

their families may have a relative from a different tradition, as well as friends from a variety of traditions.

5.2.6. Missionary Initiation

All catechesis must involve and terminate in the desire to bring about more disciples for our Lord. The *DC* states, "Catechesis... forms believers for mission, accompanying them in the maturation of attitudes of faith and making them aware that they are missionary disciples, called to participate actively in the proclamation of the Gospel and to make the Kingdom of God present in the world."[143] Furthermore, *Catechesi Tradendae* (*CT*) remarks that catechesis runs the risk of becoming barren if no community of faith and missionary life is involved.[144]

Having looked at the goals, tasks, and prospects of faith education of adolescents and youth, the following paragraphs shall consider the *faith-focused mentoring* paradigm of Vallabaraj[145] as another prospect for a holistic process of catechetical education of adolescents and youth.

5.3. Faith-Focused Mentoring as a Holistic Process for Adolescents and Youth

Faith-focused mentoring as a holistic process for the catechetical education of adolescents and youth simply means an approach that respects their psychosomatic unity. It recognizes the bond that links the human growth of young people with their spiritual growth.[146] Mentoring as a holistic paradigm, therefore, highlights the struggle for personal wholeness through the processes of facilitating, counsel-

---

[143] *DC*, n. 50.
[144] Cf. *CT*, n. 24.
[145] Cf. VALLABARAJ, *Faith-Focused Mentoring as a Paradigm for Youth Catechesis*, 295–318.
[146] Cf. VALLABARAJ, *Faith-Focused Mentoring as a Paradigm for Youth Catechesis*, 295.

ing, protecting, and coaching as an integral part of the faith education of adolescents. This is specifically for educators and youth ministers of adolescents. Vallabaraj brings out four holistic characteristics of how the lives of adolescents are dynamically and interdependently made up.[147] In this work, we therefore adopt them as an operational consideration for the faith education of adolescents as seen below.

Firstly, *it is developmental.* Following the principle of graduality, in mentoring adolescents and youth, they should be perceived from a developmental perspective, which views growth as gradual and ongoing, with the facets of struggles shifting with age and time. Such a developmental process ought not to run counter to the adolescent's readiness to advance to the next stage of the pace of God's grace.[148]

Secondly, *it is experiential.* Mentoring should touch the ever-changing concrete life situations of adolescents and youth. This is because mentoring in such life situations involves a confluent approach that brings together head, heart, and hands—the cognitive, affective, and behavioral dimensions of the adolescents.[149]

Thirdly, *it is integrative.* A holistic mentoring of adolescents and youth should be concerned with unified growth that does not develop the spirit and the mind alone while neglecting the body and the emotions or vice versa. It should promote the adolescent's autonomy without forgetting the shared vision. It should respect his/her relationships with self, others, the community, and with Jesus Christ and encourage his/her human experience.[150]

Lastly, *it is transformative.* Holistic mentoring should promote ongoing changes in the life of adolescents and youth in the community as a whole. This transformation includes continuing changes in

---

[147] Cf. VALLABARAJ, *Faith-Focused Mentoring as a Paradigm for Youth Catechesis,* 296.
[148] Cf. VALLABARAJ, *Faith-Focused Mentoring as a Paradigm for Youth Catechesis,* 298.
[149] Cf. VALLABARAJ, *Faith-Focused Mentoring as a Paradigm for Youth Catechesis,* 298.
[150] Cf. VALLABARAJ, *Faith-Focused Mentoring as a Paradigm for Youth Catechesis,* 298.

thoughts, attitudes, feelings, values, and behavior. They should be able to receive faith education that informs, forms, and transforms their lives, communities, and societies.[151]

Considering these characteristics of faith-focused mentoring of adolescents and youth will definitely be of help in the catechesis they receive and their ongoing maturation.

---

[151] Cf. VALLABARAJ, *Faith-Focused Mentoring as a Paradigm for Youth Catechesis*, 298.

CHAPTER 6

THE STRATEGY OF THE CHURCH IN MINISTERING TO ADOLESCENTS AND YOUTH

6.1. Pastoral Strategy

Given the advancement in technology and the rapid growth of the digital world, the entire Church today looks with greater attentiveness at the passage from the age of youth to that of adulthood.[152] Our Lord Jesus—who sanctified the stage of adolescence and youth by the very fact that he passed through and lived it, in meeting with children, adolescents, and young people over the course of his pastoral ministry—showed them the Father's kindness, questioned them, and invited them to a life of fullness. Following this example, therefore, the Church continues in the same light as the *DC* stipulates: The Church, manifesting the same solicitude as Jesus, wants to listen to young people with patience, understand their anxieties, have a true heart-to-heart dialogue, and accompany them in discerning their life span. The pastoral care of youth by the Church is therefore to be first of all a *humanizing and missionary outreach*, which means

---

[152] Cf. *DC*, n. 256.

being capable of seeing the signs of God's love and calling in human experience.[153] This particular quote brings out the recommendation that, in each Parish, the pastoral care of young people should be a priority of the pastor and the entire Christian community. They should be understood and listened to through the various programs carved out for them in the pastoral plan of the Parish; they should speak the language of love and closeness to them, taking into account their future and dreams; they should not judge or expect from them a perfection beyond their limits, but they should be accompanied, following the example of Christ.

In helping young people to discover, develop, and live their life plans according to God, pastoral care of adolescents and youth is to adopt new styles and strategies, especially in modern-day circumstances. As the scientific world progresses in technological and digital development with the young people of today as digital natives, so is their pastoral care, which should be constantly updated. In line with the *synodal* pastoral care of young people, Pope Francis remarks that young people make us see the need for new styles and new strategies. For example, while adults often worry about having everything properly planned, with regular meetings and fixed times, most young people today have little interest in this kind of pastoral approach.[154] In this regard, the *DC* recommends: "**It is necessary to become more flexible: inviting young people to events or occasions that provide an opportunity not only for learning, but also for conversing celebrating, singing, listening to real stories and experiencing a shared encounter with the living God.**"[155] Some of these activities can take place during youth camps, rallies, faith formation, or other occasions that are dear to the various associations of young people.

Following this strategy, therefore, various topics depending on the occasion and age groups can be chosen. It should be noted that in cases where the gatherings include young people of all ages, the principle of graduality should be respected. Different topics can be

---

[153] *DC*, n. 252.
[154] *ChV*. n. 204.
[155] *DC*, n. 252.

INTEGRAL FAITH EDUCATION OF ADOLESCENTS AND YOUTH

selected to suit the age group in question. Number 254 of *DC* brings out two types of strategies; *organic and structured catechetical programs and casual catechetical (formative) programs.*

6.2. Organic and Structured Catechetical Programs

Organic and structured catechetical programs refer to a systematic organization of formation in the Parish or institution such that it combines liturgical, spiritual, doctrinal, and moral formation to realize the two main goals of catechesis for young people which are the development of the *kerygma* and growth. By the development of the *kerygma*, we mean the foundational experience of encounter with God through Christ's death and resurrection.[156] By growth, it refers to catechesis or education that will enable young people to advance in fraternal love, community life, and service.[157] The systematic faith education of adolescents and youth is therefore to present the proclamation of the passion, death, and resurrection of Jesus, the true source of youthfulness for the world, as a core of meaning around which to build the vocational response. As the catechism of the Catholic Church explains, deepening of faith is education in the faith of children, young people, and adults that includes especially the teaching of Christian doctrine imparted, generally speaking, organically and systematically with a view of initiating the hearers into the fullness of Christian life.[158] This shows that it is in the mind of the church for catechesis to be done organically and systematically to achieve the best results. That notwithstanding, catechesis or faith education can also be done casually and flexibly according to circumstances, events, and pastoral situations.

One of the areas of organic and systematic catechetical programs is catechesis of various age groups in preparation for the sacraments of Christian initiation, most especially that of Baptism and

---

[156] Cf. *ChV*, n. 213.
[157] Cf. *ChV*, n. 213.
[158] Cf. *Catechism of the Catholic Church*, Libreria Editrice Vaticana, Vatican City 1992, n. 5.

first Holy Communion, as that of Confirmation in many Parishes will always be done at a later period following the directives and policies of each Diocese. It follows the stipulated number of years and the syllabus to be covered as determined by the catechetical office of each Diocese. **The syllabus for every age group should always take into consideration the six tasks of catechesis to give young people an integral education.**

6.3. Casual Catechetical or Educational Programs

This refers to education that is given casually in the life environments of young people be it in schools (institutions), colleges, universities; cultural and recreational associations; or during pilgrimages and many other occasions that bring young people together. This implies that, as opposed to the systematic and progressive presentation of catechesis, casual catechesis is more flexible and that topics are chosen depending on the needs, circumstances, and age group in question. These occasions come up at Parish, diocesan, national, and international levels. Worthy of note is the *World Youth Day* (WYD). In the various institutions, some periods could be set aside for casual catechesis or integral education.

6.4. Vocational Dimension of Adolescence and Youth Catechesis

It should be noted that as a formation is given to adolescents and other young people in general, particular attention should be paid to the vocational dimension of the priesthood, consecrated life, and marriage. This requires that pathways of formation be developed in reference to experiences and the specificities of the respective vocations. This implies that priests and religious and married people be invited from time to time to a Parish setup to introduce young people to the respective vocations in concrete terms. This will facilitate the atmosphere of discernment. Appreciation must be shown for the fact that often young people's journey of faith is also mediated by membership in an ecclesial association or movement. They should be encouraged to join groups with particular spiritualities and charisms that will bring about their aspirations. The group dynamic, in fact, allows catechesis to remain intimately connected to concrete experience.[159]

6.5. Some Other Strategies for Adolescents and Youth Faith Education

Considering the fact that the young people of this modern generation are digital natives, it will be most important to employ methods that can better speak to them in their language. The *DC* notes, in this connection, that new technologies have created a new cultural infrastructure that influences the communication and lives of persons and most especially that of the young people in this generation. In virtual space, which many consider no less important than the real world, people get news and information, develop and express opinions, engage in debate and dialogue, and seek answers to their questions.[160] The faith education of the young will fail to be integral and up-to-date, and as such, it risks appearing insignificant if it does not adequately consider these phenomena.[161]

Moreover, within the Church, there is often a habit of one-directional communication: preaching, teaching, and the presentation of dogmatic summaries. Looking at the young people of today, the written word alone struggles to speak to them; this is because they are used to a language consisting of a combination of written word, sound, and images.[162] In this regard, digital forms of communication offer greater possibilities for the transmission of faith to them because these forms are open to interaction. That is why as a youth minister or catechist, along with technological knowledge, it is necessary to learn effective approaches to communication that will facilitate any

---

[159] Cf. *ChV*, n. 219–220.
[160] Cf. *DC*, n. 213.
[161] Cf. *DC*, n. 213.
[162] Cf. *DC*, n. 214.

catechetical activity with the young. Some of these include the use of music, movies, comedy, arts, symbols, cartoons, and the like.

6.5.1. Use of Arts in Catechesis

According to Bill (in his article "What Is Art?"), art is the product of creative human activity in which materials are shaped or selected to convey an idea, emotion, or visually interesting form.[163] Furthermore, the word *art* can refer to the visual arts, including painting, sculpture, architecture, photography, decorative arts, crafts, and other visual works that combine materials or forms. It is the use of skill and imagination in the creation of aesthetic objects that can be shared with others. It involves the arranging of elements in a way that appeals to the senses or emotions and acts as a means of communication with the viewer as it represents the thoughts of the artist. While art is an action, the person who performs the action is known as an artist. Given this understanding of art, Pope Francis, in his Apostolic Exhortation, *The Joy of the Gospel*, touched on the use of arts in faith formation as he says:

> Each particular Church should encourage the use of the arts in evangelization, building on the treasures of the past, but also drawing upon the wide variety of contemporary expressions so as to transmit the faith in a new 'language of parables.' We must be bold enough to discover new signs and new symbols, new flesh to embody and communicate the word, and different forms of beauty which are valued in different cultural settings, including those unconventional modes of beauty which may mean little to the evangelizers, yet prove particularly attractive to others.[164]

---

[163] Bill, "What is Art? *Artscolumbia,* artscolumbia.org, 2022.
[164] *EG*, n. 167.

Consequently, creating programs that deal with virtual arts and the use of paintings that carry a doctrinal message, pictures, sculpture, the beauty of nature, architecture, Christian symbols, and the like will be more welcoming and effective to the young.

6.5.2. Music and Catechesis

Among the many signs and symbols used by the Church to celebrate its faith, music is of preeminent importance.[165] Young people love music in all forms—to sing and to dance. To evangelize through music is to speak of the love of Christ, which is the purest, most beautiful thing, in a way that everyone understands and that touches the heart. To make use of music in catechesis will be in two ways: firstly, to punctuate the time for catechesis with songs either given by talented young people or recorded music or songs with divine messages, especially in the lives of young people. The songs used can be for animation to keep them alive and active to follow the catechesis, or they could carry the message based on the topic chosen for the catechesis (after playing, some lessons can be drawn). In this regard, Jack Miffleton, a gifted teacher, a songwriter, and a youth minister, especially in children's religious education, has this testimony to share:

> It is difficult to imagine catechesis with primary and middle grade children without music, movement[,] and song. It is a natural and spontaneous way that children express themselves. Punctuating a lesson with songs and acclamations is good pedagogy, good religion, and children like it! Singing is good pedagogy. Young children have short attention spans. Movement and song are aids in helping them focus. Regular singing

---

[165] NATIONAL CONFERENCE OF CATHOLIC BISHOPS, *Music in Catholic Worship*, Washington, D.C. (1312 Massachusetts Ave., N.W., Washington 200005), 1983.

can help establish an easy rapport between catechist and child by allowing the catechist to enter the world of the child without being "childish." Singing the Scriptures adds a unique dimension to the process of hearing and learning about God's word. If students can sing it, they will remember it. Modern Catholic hymnals are filled with Scripture in song. Recorded songs or instrumental music can create an atmosphere of reverence during a quiet time or while your students are involved in individual or group projects. Singing is good religion. "One who sings, prays twice," wrote Saint Augustine. Using music in a catechetical setting is not just a practical teaching device; it is also good religious education. The liturgies of the Church are sung prayers. From the beginning, children can benefit from an approach to prayer and catechesis that is modeled on liturgy. In liturgy, for example, a verbal proclamation is usually followed by a sung response. Acclamatory song can highlight a lesson or classroom activity. Beginning and ending a class with a seasonal psalm or song refrain can draw students into the liturgical year without preaching about it. Singing is fun! An important aspect of catechesis is the socialization and friendships that take place among the children in your class or group. Singing with one voice strengthens this process of community building. Even when singing together just for fun, Christian children model what they are as one Body of Christ.[166]

---

[166] Jack MIFFLETON, "Music in Catechesis", *Oregon Catholic Press (OCP's Publications)*, www.ocp.org, 26th November 2021.

This testimonial reflection brings out four things. Firstly, it is in the nature of young people and especially preadolescents to sing and dance. Secondly, using music in catechesis is not only a pedagogical device, but it is also religious education and preparing young minds for active liturgical participation. Thirdly, it creates socialization and friendship between the teacher and students as well as among the students themselves. And finally, it strengthens community building.

6.5.3. Comedy and Catechesis

One of the methods in translating catechesis into the world of the young is by using comedy during catechetical events or activities that involve young people. To begin with, people love to laugh. Comedy makes people feel good, and at the same time, it can also expose painful truths that are just easier to laugh at. For instance, if someone is making fun of something we personally have experienced, something that is relatable, it can be hilarious. We do not always know why, but it can provide relief to look at something in a new way. It is almost healing.

According to Alyssa Maio, a screenwriter, in *StudioBinder*, "Comedy is any work that is intended to incite laughter and amusement, especially in theatre, television, film, stand-up comedy or any other entertainment medium."[167] It dates back to the Ancient Greeks, originating from the literary definition of comedy, which refers to a medieval story or narrative involving an amusing character that triumphs over poor circumstances, creating comic effects. The tone here is light and satirical, and the story always ends well.[168]

Young people face a lot of challenges in their journey in faith, social life, and family life. When these challenges and the struggles they go through are touched in any catechetical session, it sinks differently. Given that many of them are talented in theater art, comedy, and music, they can be encouraged and helped to come out with

---

[167] Cf. Alyssa MAIO, "What is Comedy?" *StudioBinder, www.studioBinder.com*, 28th November 2019.

[168] Cf. Alyssa MAIO, "What is Comedy?"

comedy, carrying divine messages and sound education in the lives of their fellow youth and their environment, as they know exactly what happens among them. Making comedy out of moral values that are inadequate in society can easily go through in a humorous way. As mentioned, when dealing with the use of music in catechesis, comedy can be punctuated with the topic in consideration and stand on its own, provided it has an educative value in the lives of adolescents and youth. Its use will bring in more young people to attend the sessions as well as keep them alive and active. Taking into consideration also that comedy, as good as it is, can also be derogatory, mocking, and sarcastic, young people are cautioned to be sensitive to the feelings of others and charitable in their use of this art.

6.5.4. Movies/Stories and Catechesis

Generally speaking, a movie or film is a type of visual communication that uses moving pictures and sound to tell stories or teach people something. Most people watch (view) movies as a form of entertainment or as a way to have fun. Furthermore, this work of visual art simulates experiences and otherwise communicates ideas, stories, perceptions, feelings, beauty, or atmosphere through the use of moving images. These images are generally accompanied by sound and, more rarely, other sensory stimulations.

With this understanding, therefore, very educative movies that paint the picture of life in the Church and society can be used as catechesis or for catechesis. It could be the lives of saints, already recorded presentations, and other movies suited for the lives of adolescents and youth. Unlike a typical movie show, the movies can be paused and other explanations and enlightenments given. At the end of the presentations, testimonies can be made and lessons drawn. Catechesis done this way will achieve a greater influence. At times, (let) the young people could act themselves and present some episodes during youth activities, and lessons drawn from them could also be a great catechesis. This will create active participation as well as promote talents in the lives of some.

The use of technical devices such as computers, projectors, TV screens, radios, sound systems (speakers and microphones), and many others can greatly facilitate the faith education of adolescents and youth. These devices speak to their world more than anything else.

The use of stories and happenings that have taken place in the environment or happenings around can be a device for catechesis. Jesus, in His divine pedagogy, used parables to pass across His message of salvation. These parables He used were earthly, well-known stories where He inserted a heavenly message. Like Jesus, we can make use of the stories familiar to young people and catechize them.

Opportunities can also be given to young people to share experiences of particular challenges in their response to their faith or conversion experiences from particular vices or life lessons realized in some challenges. These testimonies can be enough catechesis for others facing similar challenges. Care should be taken so that these testimonies are scrutinized beforehand to avoid embarrassment of any sort.

6.5.5. Use of Cartoons/Comics in Catechesis

Comic and *cartoon* are two closely interrelated words, but they do not mean the same. A comic is a publication, typically a book that consists of comic art in the form of sequentially juxtaposed panels that represent individual scenes.[169] The individual illustrations in the book may be called a cartoon, but a comic book cannot be called a cartoon. Comics use different textual devices such as balloons, captions, effects, dialogues, and other information.

On the other hand, the meaning of the word *cartoon* can have subtle differences; for instance, a cartoon can refer to a simple illustration, a style of drawing, or an animation. Principally, a cartoon is an illustration drawn in a nonrealistic or semirealistic artistic style.[170] Cartoons in print media can be classified into various categories such

---

[169] Cf. HASA, "Comic and Cartoon," *DifferenceBetween.com*, 13th December 2016.
[170] Cf. HASA, "Comic and Cartoon."

as editorial cartoons, gag cartoons, and comic strips. They are often meant to evoke humor and laughter. *Editorial cartoons* are serious in tone and use satire or irony to criticize social issues; they are often found in news publications. *Comic strips* are a short series of drawings and speech bubbles in sequence. *Gag cartoons* or panel comics consist of only one illustration and depict an everyday situation but with a twist. *Animations*, especially those that target children and evoke laughter, are also termed *cartoons*. They can be television programs or short animated movies.[171]

Flowing from the understanding of the use of comics and cartoons in the world of arts, integral faith education can make good use of these arts to catechize. The production of scriptural passages and Bible stories in comic and cartoon form can attract the younger generation. For instance, there are children's catechisms that are designed in this format. A whole catechetical session can be delivered with just one cartoon or several of them depending on the topic in consideration. As mentioned under the use of movies in catechesis, short animated movies with some moral values and scriptural background can be played, most especially for children and preadolescents. Drawings that reflect the Gospel message and create the disposition to worship God are found in some Churches. These images are catechetical, for they tell a long story in just one picture. The use of these, therefore, will be a good strategy for the integral faith education of adolescents and youth.

In conclusion, regarding digital languages and tools in catechesis, the Magisterium recommends that it is good for communities to strive not only to address new cultural challenges but also to respond to the new generations with tools that are already in common use in teaching. Furthermore, youth ministers and catechists must be aware of the extent to which the virtual world can leave profound marks on younger or more fragile persons and how much influence it can have in the management of emotions or in the construction of one's identity.[172]

---

[171] Cf. Hasa, "Comic and Cartoon."
[172] Cf. *DC*, n. 216.

CHAPTER 7

WORLD YOUTH DAY AS A PASTORAL GUIDE FOR EVERY YOUTH MINISTRY

7.1. The Importance of World Youth Day

World Youth Day (WYD) is one of the main strategies for integral faith education for young people. It is the prophetic initiative of Pope Saint John Paul II on the integral pastoral care of young people. In his words,

> All young people must feel that they are cared for by the Church. Therefore, may the entire Church on a worldwide level, in union with the Successor of Peter, be more and more committed to young people, to their concerns and worries and to their aspirations and hopes, so as to meet their expectations by communicating the certainty that is Christ, the Truth that is Christ, the love that is Christ.[173]

---

[173] JOHN PAUL II, *To the College of Cardinals and members of the Roman Curia for Christmas*, 20 December 1985.

It has *kerygmatic*, formative, witnessing, sacramental, and artistic dimensions. It is celebrated at the international level and at the diocesan level or in particular Churches. At the international level the, event is generally held every three years in a different country, each time with the presence of the Holy Father. The ordinary celebration of WYD, on the other hand, takes place every year in the particular Churches or Dioceses that undertake the organization of the event.

Pope Benedict XVI took up the baton from his predecessor. On various occasions, he stressed that these events are a providential gift for the church. He described them as "a remedy against faith fatigue," "a new, more youthful form of Christianity," and "new evangelization put into practice."[174] In Pope Francis's view, too, World Youth Day provides an extraordinarily powerful missionary thrust for the whole Church and, in particular, for the younger generations. Pope Francis clarified a central point concerning WYD by saying this: *Let us always remember: young people do not follow the Pope, they follow Jesus Christ, bearing his Cross. And the Pope guides them and accompanies them on this journey of faith and hope.*[175]

At the end of Mass on the Solemnity of Christ the King on November 22, 2020, Pope Francis called for a relaunch of the celebration of WYD in particular Churches. He announced that this celebration, which has been traditionally held on Palm Sunday, starting in 2021 will be held on the Sunday of the Solemnity of Christ the King.[176] According to the directives of the Dicastery for Laity, Family and Life, it is suggested that World Youth Day at diocesan levels be held on the same date as the Solemnity of Christ the King, including in churches where their rite does not provide for this Solemnity,

---

[174] Cf. BENEDICT XVI, *Christmas greetings to Cardinals, Archbishops, Bishops, and Directors of the Governorate of Vatican City State*, 22 December 2011.

[175] Cf. POPE FRANCIS, *Angelus*, 4 August 2013.

[176] Cf. POPE FRANCIS, *Solemnity of Our Lord Jesus Christ, King of the Universe*, 22 November 2020.

although it can be celebrated on another day. Nevertheless, Ordinaries have the faculty to decide on an alternative.[177]

The annual diocesan celebration of World Youth Day is an important event that emphasizes the role young people play in the Catholic Church. This initiative has as its motive to ensure that younger generations feel that they are at the center of the Church's attention and pastoral concern. The celebration of these youth days at a local level is, therefore, extremely useful in keeping the Church mindful of the importance of walking with young people, welcoming them, and listening to them with patience while proclaiming the word of God to them with affection and power. In other words, it is a strategy of the Church to open and improve itself, in recognizing the people who are most in need to be loved and guided while helping them to find their identity as children who belong to God. World Youth Day, by its very name and nature, is meant for every young person in the world. This implies that no one is excluded or can excuse themselves. Consequently, Church leaders and those in charge of youth ministry should do everything they can to accompany every single youth and young adult in their area. The celebration of WYD at the diocesan level is very important because of the following:

- It offers young people *a personal experience of a festival of faith*, which is especially important for those who cannot attend international events because of studies, work, or financial difficulties.
- It generates a commitment in young people that will change the face of the society in which they live and increase their sense of belonging.
- It gives young people the opportunity to foster new friendships and dialogue in the hope of a better life by resolving differences, especially with other religions.

---

[177] DICASTERY FOR LAITY, FAMILY AND LIFE, *Pastoral Guidelines for the Celebration of World Youth Day in the Particular Churches*, Vatican City, 22 April, 2021, n. 2.

- It grants young people the opportunity to experience other cultures and provides a good disposition to accommodate and learn from them.
- It helps young people, especially those who are unable to attend the international celebration or who are not active in their faith community, to know how much Christ and the Church love, support, and want to journey with them.

From the pastoral guidelines offered by the dicastery mentioned above, six catechetical cornerstones that constitute the heart of the WYD can be emphatically highlighted.

7.1.1. WYD as a Festival of Faith

It can be noted that WYD offers young people a lively and joyful experience of faith and communion, a space to experience the beauty of the face of God. Since at the heart of a life of faith is our encounter with Jesus, every WYD should resound with the invitation for each young person to meet Christ and enter into a personal dialogue with him. This is done in the context of a greater celebration, which is the feast of faith, when together, we praise the Lord, sing, listen to the word of God, and remain in the silence of worship.[178] That is, the program is creatively adapted to include particular attention to *moments of silent adoration of the Eucharist* as an act of faith par excellence and to *penitential liturgies* as a special place of encounter with God's mercy.[179]

7.1.2. Experience of the Church

The guidelines stress that WYD be an occasion for young people to experience ecclesial communion and to grow in their awareness of being an integral part of the Church.[180] To achieve this, the guidelines suggest that the first way to involve young people is to *listen to them*

---

[178] Cf. POPE FRANCIS, *General Audience*, 4th September 2013.
[179] Cf. Dicastery For Laity, Family And Life, n. 4a.
[180] Cf. Dicastery For Laity, Family And Life, n. 4b.

and find appropriate times and ways for the voices of young people to be heard within the existing structures of communion. It could be at the level of diocesan, interdiocesan, ecclesiastical provinces, presbyteral councils, or local councils of Bishops.[181] It is recommended that there should also be room for the various charisms present in the jurisdiction alongside the young people for a more participatory and co-responsible Church, where no one is excluded or excludes themselves. In this way, it will be possible to gather and coordinate all the dynamic forces of the particular Church, as well as to reawaken those that are dormant. At the same time, the presence of the local Bishop and his willingness to be among the young people show them a clear sign of love and closeness in the pastoral style of proximity. It is often the case for many young people that the diocesan celebration of WYD is an opportunity to meet and converse with their Bishop. Pope Francis encourages this pastoral style of proximity, "where we need to use above all the language of closeness, the language of generous, relational and existential love that touches the heart, impacts life, and awakens hope and desires."[182]

7.1.3. *Missionary Experience*

At the international level, WYD has proved to be an excellent opportunity for young people to have a missionary experience. Youth ministry is always *missionary*, says Pope Francis.[183] In the same vein, at the diocesan level, outreach activities and missions can be organized, which encourage young people to visit people in their homes carrying *a message of hope, a word of comfort, or simply being willing to listen*. Their enthusiasm can also be harnessed *to allow them to lead occasions of public evangelization with songs, prayer, and testimonies*. They can go to streets and squares in the city where their peers meet because young people are the best evangelizers of young people. This fulfills one of the six tasks of catechesis as previously explained. Their

---

[181] Cf. Dicastery For Laity, Family And Life, n. 4b.
[182] *ChV* n. 211.
[183] *ChV* n. 240.

very presence and their joyful faith already constitute a *living proclamation* of the Good News that attracts other young people. Also, activities in which young people have an experience of voluntary work, freely given service, and self-giving are to be encouraged. In this way, young people are offered the chance to become *protagonists of the revolution of charity and service, capable of resisting the pathologies of consumerism and superficial individualism.*[184]

7.1.4. Vocational Discernment and Call to Holiness

The pastoral guidelines encourage priority for the vocation dimension of the WYD, which aims at helping young people "understand that their whole life is placed before God who loves them and calls them. God has called them first and foremost to life and continually calls them to happiness. They are called to get to know God and to listen to his voice, and above all to accept his Son Jesus as their teacher, friend[,] and Saviour."[185] When they have come to terms with these *fundamental vocations* within the broader *vocational horizons*, young people can be proposed the choice that must be made of a state of life, one that is in accord with the call that God is addressing to each of them individually, whether it be to the priesthood or the consecrated life, including in the monastic form, or marriage and family. It will be advantageous to invite seminarians, consecrated persons, and members of societies of apostolic life that are present in the Diocese to participate and briefly portray their charisms and brochures for young people to have access to for their discernment, not leaving out the couples of the family life ministry. In fact, by their presence and witness, they can help to prompt young people to ask the right vocational questions and to desire to set out in search of the *great plan* that God has in mind for them. Meanwhile, *every vocational choice must have at its heart an even more profound call to*

---

[184] Cf. *ChV* n. 174.
[185] Dicastery For Laity, Family And Life, n. 4d.

holiness. WYD must resonate in young people the call to holiness as the true path to happiness and self-fulfillment.[186]

7.1.5. Experience of Pilgrimage

It is recommended that WYD at the diocesan level can propose specific ways for young people to have real pilgrimage experiences—ones that encourage them to leave their homes and set out on a journey, and on the way, they are introduced to the sweat and toil of the journey, the fatigue of the body, and the joy of the spirit. All this is of vital importance at present because many young people risk isolating themselves in virtual unreal worlds (far from the dusty roads and streets of the world). The document notes that it is often through a pilgrimage together that we make new friends and experience the excitement of sharing the same ideals as we look together toward a common goal with mutual support in difficulties and the joy of sharing the little we have.[187] WYD is, therefore, a great opportunity for younger generations *to explore local shrines and other significant places of popular piety*, bearing in mind that various manifestations of popular piety, especially pilgrimages, attract young people who do not readily feel at home in ecclesial structures and represent a concrete sign of their trust in God.[188] In the pastoral care of young people, outdoor activities involving displacement from their normal and familiar environments are very much appealing to the young because they always want opportunities that will lead them to encounter other young people and new places. They are pilgrim people. It is beautifully put thus:

> They are a united people, pilgrims who 'walk together' towards a goal, towards an encounter with the One who can give meaning

---

[186] Cf. POPE FRANCIS, Apostolic Exhortation *Gaudete et Exsultate: On the Call to Holiness in Today's World*, Vatican City, 19th March 2018, n. 2.
[187] Cf. Dicastery For Laity, Family And Life, n. 4e.
[188] Cf. *ChV* n. 238.

to their existence, the God who became one of us and who calls every young person to be a disciple, to leave everything and to follow. Pilgrimage requires a minimalist approach that asks young people to leave behind empty comforts and certainties, to adopt a style of travel that is sober and welcoming and open to Providence and to "God's surprises", a style that teaches them to go beyond themselves and to face the challenges that arise along the way.[189]

In brief, pilgrimages are opportunities for young people to encounter God as well as to encounter new friends and new environments.

7.1.6. Universal Fraternity

While emphasizing the importance of involving young people in all steps of the pastoral planning for the WYD, the guidelines recommend that the testimony and experience of young people who have previously taken part in an international WYD deserve to be highlighted in the preparation at the diocesan level.[190] Very often in most Parishes, inactive and indifferent young people are excluded from participating in activities, but the guidelines encourage Dioceses to ensure that young people who are less present and less active in established pastoral structures do not feel excluded so that they feel *expected and welcomed, each one in their individual uniqueness and human and spiritual potential.* Following this way, the diocesan event can be a very good opportunity to motivate and welcome all those young people who may be looking for their place in the Church and who have not yet found it. According to Pope Francis in *ChV,* we need to build a "youth ministry capable of being inclusive, with

---

[189] Dicastery For Laity, Family And Life, n. 4e.
[190] Cf. Dicastery For Laity, Family And Life, n. 5.

room for all kinds of young people, to show that we are a Church with open doors."[191]

7.2. Cooperation with Youth Leaders

As already mentioned, youth ministry workers need to be increasingly attentive to involving young people in all the steps of pastoral planning for WYD and other activities that involve them. The synodal-missionary style is the best because it makes the most of the creativity, language, and methods typical of that age bracket. Who knows the language and the problems of their peers better than they do? Who is more capable of reaching out to them through art, social media, and the like? Of course, young people are the best apostles to fellow young people.

7.3. Icons of WYD

7.3.1. *WYD Cross*

The World Youth Day cross has many names: Jubilee Cross, Pilgrim Cross, and Youth Cross. It was entrusted to the youth as they were given the commission to *"carry it throughout the world as a symbol of Christ's love for humanity, and announce to everyone that only in the death and resurrection of Christ can we find salvation and redemption."*[192] The cross was set out with the young people from Saint Peter's in 1984 and has since been carried around the world, making a pilgrimage from Parish to Parish, Diocese to Diocese, and country to country.

---

[191] *ChV*, n. 234.
[192] JOHN PAUL II, Palm Sunday, Rome, 1984.

7.3.2. WYD Icon

On the same occasion, Pope John Paul II entrusted to the youth an icon of the blessed mother that would accompany the cross. *"It will be a sign of Mary's motherly presence close to young people who are called, like the Apostle John, to welcome her into their lives."*[193] So the cross and icon are carried together through the world, touching hearts and inspiring holiness. There are countless testimonies from people who have encountered the pilgrim cross and icon.

7.4. Message of the WYD

Traditionally, every year, prior to the diocesan celebration of WYD, the Holy Father publishes a message for young people. This message is an appropriate guide for the preparatory meetings of WYD at the diocesan level. It is expected that this message with its biblical and magisterial text be explained and applied to the actual real-life circumstances that these particular young people are encountering. This work of mediation, carried out in catechesis and dialogue, will also help young people to identify specific ways in which to bear witness to the Word of God that they have heard, to live it out in their daily lives, and to embody it at home, in their places of work or study, and among friends.[194] It is also important for young people to hear the Word of God and the word of the Church firsthand from people close to them—people who are familiar with their characteristics, history, tastes, difficulties and struggles, expectations, and hopes.

The direction proposed by the Pope's message, which is intended to accompany the journey of the universal Church with young people, can therefore be interpreted with intelligence and great cultural sensitivity by taking into account the local context. It could also inspire the path of youth ministry in the local Church while not forgetting the two main lines of action that Pope Francis has iden-

---

[193] JOHN PAUL II, Palm Sunday, Rome, 1984.
[194] Cf. Dicastery For Laity, Family And Life, n. 6.

tified: outreach and growth.[195] The message could also be conveyed through various artistic expressions or initiatives of a social nature, as Pope Francis says, "Offer the world, the Church[,] and other young people something beautiful, whether in the realm of the spirit, the arts[,] or society."[196]

It is recommended as well that the content of the message could also be taken up in other significant moments during the pastoral year, such as Youth Mission Month or the months devoted to the Word of God or to vocations, always taking into account the indications given by the respective episcopal conferences. Lastly, the message could become the theme of various other gatherings for young people that are proposed by those working in youth ministry for the local Church in the various Dioceses and Parishes.[197]

7.5. Youth Festival

It is a set of cultural, religious, and sporting events carried out by WYD pilgrims in a sharing of the Christian experience made by young people from all over the world, the result of their creativity, and generosity. According to Lily Ruha, a youth festival typically is a themed event that has a wide variety of activities for young people. Common festival themes include art, music, dance, film, games, academics, and social and religious topics. Some festivals require auditions and applications for performance and/or participation.[198]

A large youth festival that focuses on dance might expose young people to multiple styles of dance or might focus on a specific type of dancing. A youth film festival usually spotlights films created by young people on a variety of themes, including peer pressure, sexuality, abuse, or popular culture. An academic youth festival typically focuses on a specific academic subject and allows young people to

---

[195] Cf. *ChV*, n. 209.
[196] POPE FRANCIS, Message for the 35th World Youth Day 2020.
[197] Cf. Dicastery For Laity, Family And Life, n. 6.
[198] Lily RUHA, "What is a Youth Festival," in *https://www.wisetour.com/what-is-a-youth-festival.htm*, 25th November 2022.

immerse themselves in the topic. Cultural exchange is one of the focuses of some youth festivals.[199] In the context of WYD, a youth festival provides pilgrims with an experience of joy, youth, universality, and faith, showing that the Catholic Church is lively and young, capable of using the language of all forms of arts in the work of evangelization.

7.6. Pastoral Guide for Youth Ministry

A careful study of the guidelines proposed by the Dicastery for Laity, Family and Life, as examined above, though with reference to WYD at the diocesan level, brings out the pastoral strategy of youth ministry that is to be observed in all Dioceses for all activities involving young people. In brief, it is a pastoral guide for youth ministry. It contains the *kerygmatic*, formative, witnessing, sacramental, and artistic dimensions of youth ministry. This means that any chaplain or youth worker, be it at the diocesan or Parish level, should come up with youth programs that reflect these cornerstones discussed above. It should not be forgotten that "the Church has so much to talk about with youth, and youth have so much to share with the Church."[200]

The pastoral guidelines are a great resource that presents the ideal motivations and possible practical implementations that will allow the youth ministry to be an opportunity to bring out the potential for good that is in each young person, with their generosity, thirst for authentic values, and great ideals. *To invest in young people is to invest in the future of the Church*. It is about encouraging vocation, and it effectively means the initiation of remote preparation for the families of tomorrow. It is, therefore, a vital task for every local Church and not simply one more activity. This leads us to the last and very important chapter of this book—*the necessity of suitable environments for adolescents and youth*.

---

[199] Lily RUHA, "What is a Youth Festival."
[200] JOHN PAUL II, Post-Synodal Apostolic Exhortation *Christi fideles Laici*, Vatican City, 30th December 1988, n. 46.

CHAPTER 8

THE NECESSITY OF SUITABLE ENVIRONMENTS FOR ADOLESCENTS AND YOUTH

8.1. The Priority of the Pastoral Care of Young People

In the words of Saint John Paul II, "The pastoral care of youth must clearly be a part of the overall pastoral plan of Dioceses and Parishes, so that young people will be enabled to discover very early on the value of the gift of self, an essential means for the person to reach maturity."[201] The integral formation of the young people in the Church, therefore, is a necessity that not only prepares them for the future but also fulfills the mission of the Church to nurture every member of Christ's body—the Church. This implies that every pastoral institution that does not take into consideration the integral faith education of the young is making a grave mistake. To invest in young people is to invest in the future of the Church and society. It becomes very urgent, especially in the challenging circumstances of the present-day Church and society and the increasing advancement in technology in which young people are most involved. Young

---

[201] *EA*, n. 93.

people of all age groups need guidance and support as they navigate through the most challenging part of their development and seek to grow in their walk with Christ. Just like every seed needs good ground to grow, so do young people need suitable environments for growth. In other words, there is a need for various and suitable pastoral structures for adolescents and youth.

Let us make this survey by asking these compelling questions: How many youth empowerment centers do we have constructed and equipped as a home where young people can feel free and receive formation according to their various age groups? How many Dioceses, Parishes, Churches, towns, and villages have centers that facilitate integral formation of young people? For those that have the facilities, is there any budget allocated for youth formation and resources to enhance it? These are questions to be answered, and the answer will determine where and how far one is to reach the target. It is the wish of the Magisterium that suitable environments be provided for young people in all pastoral structures of the Church. This is echoed in clear terms in *Christus Vivit* number 218.

Our institutions should provide young people with places they can make their own and where they can come and go freely, feel welcome, and readily meet other young people, whether at times of difficulty and frustration or of joy and celebration. Some of this is already happening in oratories and other youth centers, which, in many cases, offer a friendly and relaxed setting where friendships can grow and where young men and women can meet one another and share not only music, games, and sports but also reflection and prayer. In such places, much can be offered without great expenditure of funds. Then, too, the person-to-person contact indispensable for passing on the message can happen, something whose place cannot be taken by any pastoral resource or strategy.[202]

When we look at this recommendation of Pope Francis on behalf of the Church and the reality that exists in Dioceses, Parishes, and Churches, we can now understand how close or how far we still

---

[202] *ChV*, n. 218.

have to travel to reach the targeted line. Sadly, the Magisterium realizes that "many young people today feel that they have inherited the failed dreams of their parents and grandparents, dreams betrayed by injustice, social violence, selfishness[,] and lack of concern for others."[203] These experiences may create a certain uncomfortable disposition. In a word, they feel uprooted. If the young grow up in a world of ashes, it will be hard for them to keep alive the flame of great dreams and projects. If they grow up in a desert devoid of meaning, where will they develop a desire to devote their lives to sowing seeds? The experience of discontinuity, uprootedness, and the collapse of fundamental certainties, fostered by today's media culture, creates a deep sense of orphanhood to which we must respond by creating an attractive and fraternal environment where others can live with a sense of purpose. This will be a great investment that pays off in the lives of the young people after.

8.2. What Is a Youth Center or Oratory Meant For?

1. A place where children's, adolescent, and youth catechesis takes place at various times
2. A place where young people acquire skills in all aspects of life that will benefit them in the Church and society
3. A place of vocational training where young people can be introduced to or receive an education that prepares them for the job market
4. A place where young people have opportunities to experience activities of voluntary work, freely given service, and self-giving that will permit them to become protagonists of the revolution of charity and service in the Church and society.
5. A place where sporting activities take place.
6. A place where music and career development take place.
7. A place of reflection and prayer.

---

[203] *ChV*, n. 216.

8. A place of encounter.
9. Summarily in the words of Saint John Bosco, it is a home, a Church, a school, and a playground.

8.3. Testimony and Way Forward

Permit me to share my observations in the pastoral care of young people, especially regarding the necessity of an environment for the young. Most Parishes in the Dioceses in Cameroon (Africa) do have a Church where the mysteries of our salvation are celebrated, and in some places, it is the only meeting place (structure) for all Christians. In addition to the main Church in some Parishes, there is a Blessed Sacrament Chapel for Eucharistic adoration and other silent prayers for Christians. Some have halls for gatherings and group meetings; these halls are open to all Christians to use. At the same time, they are technically restricted, for they are more of an income-generating unit where those who are in need can pay and use. Most have a primary school (elementary school) where children begin their primary studies. There is often a presbytery (rectory) where priests live and minister to the Parishioners. There are many Church groups and associations in the Parish that need places to effectively carry out their activities but are not opportune because of a lack of space and finances to procure these places. Given that there are these groups and the Parish has an obligation to create avenues for group meetings, there is one area that is of utmost importance. This area is **an oratory** or **a youth center** for the integral formation of young people. This is because, as mentioned already, investing in young people is investing in the future of the Parish and society. And as a strategy of the universal Church, like Jesus did, the Church wants to listen to young people with patience, understand their anxieties, have a true heart-to-heart dialogue, and accompany them in discerning their life span.

As there is a great need for a primary school or elementary school in each Parish to take care of children who may not be able to move far away for security reasons to procure elementary knowledge, there is an even greater need for a place of formation in all directions

INTEGRAL FAITH EDUCATION OF ADOLESCENTS AND YOUTH

for all young people according to their age groups in Parishes and Churches. When these young people finish their primary education, for instance, some or most of them move to other areas, even far away from home, to continue their studies. Furthermore, in these institutions, the target program of studies is mostly academic in view of certification and not a fruitful and integral life in the Church and society. After the reception of the sacraments of Christian initiation, most children and young people do not frequent Church activities anymore. This is partly because the traditional methods used by all Christians do not fit their language or their world or *youth culture*. Some feel their needs are not attended to, and as such, they do not feel belonging. They prefer to go to places that will satisfy their needs and inclinations, as earlier explained in chapters 4 and 6. This is the more reason youth centers and oratories are necessary to offer an environment that can attend to their needs, and where ongoing formation will take place.

Come to think of it, these young persons (who are not specifically catered for in some institutions) are expected to lead the Church and society tomorrow. Moreover, how effective, even, was the catechesis received in preparation for the sacraments, and for how long? A lot can be achieved if these centers exist in the Parishes. The meeting of young people according to their age groups and from different institutions and with talents will bring about an unfathomable wealth of experiences and growth. A stable and systematic program of casual formation on life's issues by resource persons at suitable times for the various groups of young people will be a great investment for the society, the Parish, and the Church at large. There are so many successful and talented young people who can share their successes and talents with their peers (remember, young people are agents of youth ministry). At the same time, it becomes an avenue where experienced adults in various disciplines can share their knowledge and offer services to young people.

Young people can spend lots of time in schools and other places, but an hour spent in a youth center in an enriching program can change their lives forever. It is all about the quality of the programs (in a youth culture manner) put in place and made available for all. To realize this great necessity requires the following:

- Train youth animators or youth ministers with a good mastery of the developmental stages, world, and language of young people in some of the areas that have been outlined in this work.
- Construct youth centers or oratories with departments that can cater to youth catechesis and music, computer education, seminars, and sociocultural and sporting activities in all Parishes. Or at least make provision for a stable meeting place that can favor group activities even of small groups.
- Draw up an integral formation program that runs for the whole year with various activities according to age groups. This program should be stable and open to parents to at least know what is happening to their children and make better proposals, especially during weekends and holiday periods. The program should be flexible to accommodate adjustments.
- It should be a Parish affair and not only the affair of the priests in the Parish or youth ministers.
- It should be budgeted for and supported by all families in the Parish. For instance, there could be an annual contribution by each family for the running of the center to ensure sustainability. Imagine that each family contributes one thousand frs or two thousand frs (twenty dollars or twenty pounds euros more or less) every year, that will give quite some good money for the salaries of workers (allowances) in the centers and other formative material. These, together with other avenues of income, can establish a stable system of sustainability and self-reliance throughout the entire life of the Parish.
- Employ competent and talented youth ministers to work permanently in these institutions.

- The place of a chaplain/youth minister is absolutely important in every Parish to coordinate all youth activities and age groups alongside the other youth leaders.

With the presence of these structures in Parishes, a bigger center for diocesan activities with a chaplain and competent youth ministers can also exist at that level to oversee the formation program in all Parishes. The existence of these pastoral structures will give an opportunity for young people to be given formation in the manner recommended by the Church and reflected on in this research work.

8.1.1. The Role of the Community

The community has an important role in the accompaniment of young people; it should feel collectively responsible for accepting, motivating, encouraging, and challenging them. All should regard young people with understanding, appreciation, and affection and avoid constantly judging them or demanding of them perfection beyond their years.[204] The community should support young people financially to realize their projects in the Parish and at other levels. The community should also recognize persons who can accompany young people and encourage them to volunteer in various aspects. Parents should register their children for the formation programs and see to it that they participate.

8.1.2. Qualities of Youth Ministers

There are quite a number of qualities for youth ministers for an integral formation of young people. During the synod on young people that took place in October 2018 in the Vatican, young people suggested the following qualities. A youth minister should be

- someone who is a faithful Christian who engages with the Church and the world;

---

[204] Cf. Francis *Christus Vivit*, n. 243.

- someone who constantly seeks holiness;
- someone who is a confidant without judging;
- someone who actively listens to the needs of young people and responds in kind;
- someone deeply loving and self-aware;
- someone who recognizes his or her limits and knows the joys and sorrows of the spiritual journey;
- someone who speaks the language of closeness and of generous, relational, and existential love that touches the heart, impacts life, and awakens hope and desires in them, taking into account their future and dreams without judging or expecting from them perfection beyond their limits but accompanying them, following the example of Christ; and
- someone who acknowledges his/her own humanity—that is, the fact that they are human beings who make mistakes: not perfect people but forgiven sinners. This is a very important quality in a mentor.

Flowing from this last point, sometimes mentors are put on a pedestal, and when they fall, it may have a devastating impact on young people's ability to continue to engage in Parish activities or with the Church as a whole. Mentors should not lead young people as passive followers, but they should walk alongside them, allowing them to be active participants in the journey. They should respect the freedom that comes with a young person's process of discernment and equip them with tools to do so well. A mentor should believe wholeheartedly in a young person's ability to participate in the life of the Church. A mentor should therefore nurture the seeds of faith in young people, without expecting to immediately see the fruits of the work of the Holy Spirit. This role is not and cannot be limited to priests and members of consecrated life, but the laity should also be empowered to take on such a role. All such, mentors should benefit from being well-formed, and engage in ongoing formation.[205]

---

[205] Ibid n. 246.

8.1.3. Two Main Courses of Action in the Youth Ministry

The two main courses of action in youth ministry, as recommended by *Christus Vivit*, are *outreach*, meaning the way we attract young people to the Lord, and *growth*, the way we help those who have already had that experience to mature in it[206]. Looking at these two actions with my little experience in the life of young people in some Parishes in Latin America, the United States of America, Europe, and Africa, I realized that each region has its own predominant action and needs.

In most Parishes in Europe and America, you will realize that some facilities and centers or oratories favor the growth of youth formation, ranging from finances, personnel, and structures, but *outreach* is more of a problem in most Parishes. It is not easy to have young people gather as often as possible or for constant formation programs sometimes because of the environment and the indifference exhibited by some young people and families. Immediately after the reception of the sacraments of Christian initiation, which is done mostly in childhood and early years of preadolescence, you will hardly find them anymore. Some of the difficulties include indifference, lack of witness from the family and encouragement, other areas of recreation becoming a priority, insecurity, and lack of freedom to attend activities. Most parents are working, and more to that, children cannot go out on their own to attend activities without the supervision of parents or without parents dropping them off and picking them up, and since they cannot do that because of their work schedule, the children will be left home, especially during holiday periods. This is why outreach is a problem.

One of the problems is the inadequate catechetical knowledge of some volunteers in faith formation. Often, many will sign up for catechesis but have limited knowledge and specific material to help them with the particular age group they teach. Sometimes, they just

---

[206] Cf. FRANCIS *Christus Vivit*, Post-Synodal Apostolic Exhortation to Young People and to the entire People of God, Vatican City, Libreria Editrice Vaticana, 2019, n. 72–73.

help to occupy the children and distract them from their computers, phones, and iPads (which are part and parcel of their lives) with some recreational activities. The lack of catechists and competence and insufficient catechetical materials is not only a problem for these regions but also a general problem.

On the other hand, regarding growth, there are very good programs for faith formation and *life teen* programs for young people in some Parishes in (Europe and America) following the principle of graduality (age groups). These programs are mostly on weekends and some days during the week in the evening period. Some parents are very faithful and committed to ensuring the Christian education of their children even when some of these children do not like it. Very often, when talking with some of the teenagers, they will be honest to tell you that they are forced to attend the programs. Some, when brought to celebrate the sacrament of confession, will honestly tell you (when socializing with them) that their reason for accepting to come is bait for their parents to provide for their needs when asked. That notwithstanding, there are others who will not let their parents rest until they take them for faith formation classes and confessions. You also find a good number of volunteers who sign in to offer services in the various grades of faith formation as organized by the Parish.

Parishes in Latin American countries like those in Europe and America share the same pastoral situation but have fewer outreach difficulties as they turn out (young people) for events and youth programs are slightly improved (notwithstanding their uniqueness). According to the conclusions of the General Conference of the Latin American and Caribbean Bishops (2007), *adolescents and youth constitute the great majority of the population.*[207] They are *the hope and wealth of the continent.*[208] Their active participation is recognized in most communities. The hosting of the 2019 international WYD in Panama was a great booster in the pastoral care of adolescents

---

[207] Cf. *DA*, n. 443.
[208] Cf. *DA*, n. 554.

and youth in most Parishes. This positive impact was felt from the moment when the announcement was made to the actual hosting and afterward. The principle of graduality is respected on this continent, just as it is in Europe and America. Parishes organize the faith formation of adolescents according to grades. The group that is rarely found in these two continents is that of youth, as they are preoccupied with other areas. They seem to be very indifferent to Church activities. The best strategy for catechesis is *popular youth ministry*, as well as other strategies outlined in chapter 6.

In most African countries, especially Cameroon and the Ecclesiastical Province of Bamenda, *outreach* is not a problem. This is because you will find hundreds and thousands of young people attending activities, most especially events such as rallies, youth camps, World Youth Day celebrations, and other peculiar celebrations. In Parishes, you will find them available for Church activities. Most young people have freedom and little supervision from their parents, as opposed to the case in the western world. They just need to hear that there is a youth event somewhere, and they will attend in their numbers alongside their friends. What they lack is the finances, the personnel, and most especially the structures that will facilitate *growth* and other formative activities. This is the more reason suitable environments need to be created for them in their Parishes.

Furthermore, with the great turnout in activities of young people in most Parishes in Africa, there is limited personnel to cater to them. The burden of the work seems to be left to the chaplains and few individuals that assist with little or no training in youth ministry. The work becomes less effective as age groups are not always respected in most Parishes, as all participants are most often put in one hall for input. This is due in part to a lack of resource persons and structures to accommodate the great numbers.

More challenging is the fact that during the celebration of WYD at diocesan levels, with the great turnout in the Dioceses of the Ecclesiastical Province of Bamenda, what predominates the minds of young people is competitions and games (even with the catechesis and spiritual activities put in place), such that during the time allocated for the catechesis, most young people are not attentive as they are either preparing for the competition or wishing it finished fast so that they could get to exciting programs. These competitions are important, but the problem is that WYD is the only major formative program, and as the young people go back, they may not have such in their Parishes. Had it been they had structures and resource persons to constantly carry out these activities, the situation could be much better.

Notwithstanding, a good number of young people participate consciously, actively, and fruitfully in the celebration of sacraments, especially the Sacrament of Reconciliation. I remember very often sitting in the confessional for long hours because of the great desire for that sacrament by the young people during my five years as a diocesan youth chaplain and vocation's director for my Archdiocese from 2014 to 2019. Throughout each of these years, I organized WYD at the diocesan level and participated in some WYDs at the international level. Great conversion experiences are always being reported by young people for participating in this gathering. I admired as well the commitment and devotion of young people when it comes to Eucharistic adoration, with their beautiful songs of worship and adoration. Their strong spiritual life is a testimony of good formation from their parents and Christian communities. Imagine the impact young people from good Christian backgrounds can have on those from poor Christian backgrounds if these young people constantly come together in a center.

I also noted that with the great turnout, if all activities are halted for a few days during WYD and priority is given to that youth gathering, the great number of priests, consecrated men and women, and other resource persons can divide the great number into smaller groups following their ages, groups, and competence, and much can be realized. Allowing them all to go to one person or fewer priests will yield fewer fruits. It will be the best thing if all Parishes and institutions are led by their priests or youth chaplains to the venue of the WYD at the diocesan level.

Coming back to the analysis of the two main objectives of youth catechesis as outlined in *Christus Vivit* and as echoed in the *Directory for Catechesis*, there is still more to comment. These objectives state that every project of formation, which combines liturgical, spiritual, doctrinal, and moral formation, is to have two main goals. The first is the development of the **kerygma**, which is the foundational experience of encounter with God through Christ's death and resurrection. And the second is **growth** in fraternal love, community life, and service.[209]

Looking at these two goals, one will realize that they all have their background. The development of the *kerygma* is more of a transmission of the doctrine to the young so that they can know the Good News and continue in their daily struggle for conversion. Secondly, the goal of growth has to do with love of one another, a better life in the community, and service to the Church and society. The other side of growth, which is not explicitly mentioned, is the human experience of young people. This is made up of the challenges they face as individuals in their reception and internalization of the message, the challenges from their families, and the environment in which they live, as well as the challenges they face internally in their developmental process. No one may see the tensions within them, and what they may encounter is the judgment meted out on them for actions committed in their struggle. These are areas that preoccupy the minds of young people more. As such, they need people in their lives to guide them in this growth process.

In a group, a young person may feel secure, but as an individual, he/she goes through a lot that is happening within. Although the young may sometimes enjoy the support of their families and friends, they have to rely on themselves and their consciences and, frequently (and decisively), assume responsibility for their destiny. Good and evil, grace and sin, life and death will more and more confront one another within them, not just as moral categories but chiefly as fundamental options, which they must accept or reject lucidly, conscious of their responsibility.[210]

---

[209] Cf. PONTIFICAL COUNCIL FOR PROMOTING NEW EVANGELIZATION, *Directory for Catechesis*, n. 253.
[210] Cf. JOHN PAUL II, *Catechesi Tradendae, Apostolic Exhortation on Catechesis Today*, 16 October 1979, Vatican City, Libreria Editrice Vaticana 1979, n. 39

As mentioned already, inasmuch as we hand on the doctrine to the young people, great attention needs to be paid to their response to the teaching they receive. In response to their faith, they encounter a number of challenges in all age groups. Their problems stem from physical and psychological developments, tensions within and without, challenges of their particular stage of life, religious experience, sociocultural and political situations, economical factors, educational methodology, and personal problems. Most importantly, the problem of religious experience looms so high as indicated in the new *Directory for Catechesis*, such as lack of witnesses, lack of credibility, lack of spiritual and moral support on the part of the family, lack of accompaniment, inadequate catechesis, and a Christian community that prioritizes their formation.[211] This points to the fact that a suitable environment is needed for the pastoral care of the young in Parishes and institutions besides school activities (that are more often preoccupied with exams and little or nothing on the highlighted areas above). Various complaints can be seen in social media and forums about the political situation in various countries, about leadership in society, about management in Church and in various establishments, and about the misconduct of young people. There will be no better way to change these unless new programs are designed to cater to these needs in society. The *See, Judge, and Act* method can be employed in these institutions and similar ones for a change to be realized in the Church and society. It is only then that the common cliché you hear in speeches that young people are the hope of society and the Church will become a reality. Mahatma Gandhi used to say: *Be the change you want to see in the world.* Young people can be helped in various centers and oratories to identify the problems in the Church, in society, and in the various segments of society so as to better confront them using the *see, judge, and act* method of inquiries. As the novitiate is important for religious life and the seminary is for the ordained ministry, so is the youth ministry for an effective Christian life as well as a better life in society.

---

[211] Cf. PONTIFICAL COUNCIL FOR PROMOTING NEW EVANGELIZATION, *Directory for Catechesis*, n. 251.

CONCLUSION

The general objective of this work has been to study the principle of graduality in the integral faith education of adolescents and youth. The work has so far established that the principle of graduality historically came to the forefront of Catholic moral and pastoral theology. It stipulates that people should be encouraged to grow closer to God and his plan for their lives in a step-by-step manner rather than expecting to jump from initial conversion to perfection in a single step. This further means that genuine conversion necessarily places us on a course that intends steady progress (notwithstanding human weakness and occasional moral failures) toward an ever more consistent and holistic embrace of the truth of Christ's moral teaching. This principle is also applicable in the pedagogical realm, especially in the fields of psychology, linguistics, and didactics, from the point of view of systematic gradual growth and the content taught. Human development bears testimony that life is progressive, and as such, human undertakings can be seen from this same perspective.

The category in the realm of the young chosen has been adolescents and youths, who are divided into early adolescents (ten to thirteen), middle adolescents (fourteen to seventeen), and late adolescents (eighteen and twenty-one). After the period of adolescence is the youth stage from twenty-two to thirty years. Adolescence is a period of a progressive transition from childhood to adulthood. The foregone study has also made clear that the principle of graduality is linked to the three domains of learning: cognitive, affective, and behavioral. With the help of Thomas Groome, it is understood that the purpose of Christian religious education is a lived Christian faith. And that this Christian faith embodied in human existence calls for three activities: believing, trusting, and doing.[212] This also (in a similar fashion) links to the three ways: the way of the head, the way of the heart, and the way of the hands.[213] Together, the four dimensions of integral faith education—that is, the spiritual (soul), the human (base), the intellectual (means), and the apostolic (goal) dimensions—bring out a picture of faith education that is holistic, that is, involving the total human person.

From this study, therefore, the following proposals for the catechesis of adolescents and youth can be highlighted:

Firstly, the best means of integral faith education for adolescents and youth is the principle of graduality, suggesting that in the Parish and diocesan catechesis of adolescents and youth, they should be divided into groups of early adolescents, middle adolescents, late adolescents, and youth. This division can continue in the same light as young adulthood, middle adulthood, and late adulthood. This division, which takes into consideration the changes in the physical, cognitive, and emotional aspects, will provide a favorable ground for the effective translation of catechesis into their world. The results or the fruits will be a thousandfold. Take, for instance, the only source of catechesis gotten in some Parishes is homilies on weekdays and Sundays, and they are addressed generally to everyone. Not every priest or preacher will take into consideration the various age groups and mental capacities present in the liturgical celebration. Children, adolescents, young people, and adults each have their specificities and challenges that need to be addressed uniquely. It is only with respect to the principle of graduality and its division that we can bear much fruits, fruits that will last.

Secondly, the faith education of adolescents and youth should be integral, that is, taking into consideration the four main areas of Christian living: spiritual life, human development, knowledge of the faith, and apostolic activity. This is because these areas are like

---

[212] Cf. GROOME, *Christian Religious Education*, 77.
[213] Cf. GROOME, *Will there be Faith*, 111.

the four wheels of a car: if one of them is flat, the whole vehicle has to crawl along. With an integral faith education, the entire life of an adolescent will be directed toward Christ, who is his final end.

Thirdly, as a follow-up to integral faith education of adolescents and youth, we adopt the recommendation of Jerome Vallabaraj on *Faith-Focused Mentoring*[214] as a holistic process in the catechetical education of young people that respects their psychosomatic unity. It is our hope that with its processes of facilitating, counseling, protecting, and coaching—together with the holistic developmental, experiential, integrative, and transformative characteristics—the adolescents and youth will be initiated to view growth as a holistic and lifelong commitment.

Fourthly, in communicating the faith to adolescents and youth, their world and language, especially in the aspects of technology and social media, should be taken into consideration and catechesis translated into them; that the principles of effective communication, such as clarity, appropriate language, attention, feedback, and flexibility, should be employed; that their catechesis should be open to a variety of communicative languages and strategies, such as symbol, testimony, celebration, art, mediatic communication, and the use of music, movies, cartoon, and comedy, rather than that which is limited to catechism and purely verbal transmission. Educators should always note that young people themselves know and understand their world and language best and how to find appealing ways to come together. They know how to organize events, such as sports competitions, and ways to evangelize using social media, through text messages, songs, videos, and other ways. They should be encouraged and given the freedom to be motivated about evangelizing other young people wherever they are to be found.

Finally, in educating adolescents and youth in the faith, the three domains of learning—cognitive, affective, and behavioral—should be taken into consideration. This is because there are different categories of young people, like other learners, who have varying needs,

---

[214] VALLABARAJ, *Faith-Focused Mentoring as a Paradigm for Youth Catechesis*, 295–318.

and as such, different methods must be adopted in the planning and delivery of lessons to ensure that such needs are addressed. The three domains are linked also to the ways of the head, the heart, and the hands. This implies that every piece of knowledge should inform, form, and transform the person, and the community or environment where the person is should feel the effects of fraternal love, community life, and service. The principle of graduality can be applied to all processes of life, including formation in general and activities.

We cannot claim that we have exhausted this topic, for there are so many areas in the life of adolescents and youth that are just mentioned in this work, and their details are beyond the methodology adopted for this book. One of the areas that touch on the principle of graduality in the lives of young people is how applicable this principle is in social media which is part and parcel of the life of adolescents as well as the present generation who are *digital natives*.[215] This is because in catechesis and in the school curriculum, the principle of graduality can be respected, but it is a great challenge in the social media sphere. David Buckingham in the second chapter of his book, *The Media Education Manifesto*, addresses a wider issue about the role of the media in the lives of adolescents, namely, whether the media are good or bad for them.[216] And looking at the insufficient media education, he contends that the Internet should be treated as a basic public utility like clean water and air, and as such, it should be regulated more tightly. Companies like Facebook and Google should, in his view, be seen as media companies, not merely technology companies.[217] To him, media literacy is not simply a matter of knowing how to use particular devices, whether to access or create media messages. It must also entail an in-depth critical understanding of how these media work, how they communicate, how they represent the

---

[215] David BUCKINGHAM, *Is there a Digital Generation?* In Rebekah Willet (ed), *Digital Generations, Children, Young people and New media*, Lawrence Erlbaum Associates, London, 2006. 8.

[216] David BUCKINGHAM, *The Media Education Manifesto*, Polity Press, Cambridge, 2019, 3.

[217] BUCKINGHAM, *The Media Education Manifesto*, 124.

world, and how they are produced and used.[218] Without regulations, adolescents in particular can get anything they want from the media irrespective of their age. This is one of the challenges that this book is limited to handle at the moment, but the research shall be continued in this and other areas touching on the integral faith education of adolescents and youth.

As a conclusive admonition to adolescents and youth themselves—do not journey through life alone; be open and listen to the advice of the elders, especially in taking major life decisions; observe situations, judge, and take the right actions; do not settle for mediocrity and make the best of your talents and youthfulness; do not be discouraged by the challenges you must face; be prudent with the use of social media and listen more to the voice of God in you; and embrace the language of love for everyone; in this way, you will create a better world for yourself and others.

---

[218] BUCKINGHAM, *The Media Education Manifesto*, 124–128.

BIBLIOGRAPHY

MAGISTERIAL DOCUMENTS

Catechism of the Catholic Church, Vatican City, Libreria Editrice Vaticana, 1992.

BENEDICT XVI, *Christmas greetings to Cardinals, Archbishops, Bishops and Directors of the Governorate of Vatican City State*, 22 December 2011.

FRANCIS, *Evangelii Gaudium. Apostolic Exhortation on the Proclamation of the Gospel in Today's World*, Vatican City, Libreria Editrice Vaticana, 2013.

FRANCIS, *Christus Vivit. Post-Synodal Apostolic Exhortation to Young People and to the People of God*, Vatican City, Libreria Editrice Vaticana, 2019.

FRANCIS, *Gaudete et Exsultate*. Apostolic Exhortation *on the Call to Holiness in Today's World*, Vatican City, Libreria Editrice Vaticana, 2018.

FRANCIS, *Angelus*, 4 August 2013.

FRANCIS, *General Audience*, 4th September 2013.

FRANCIS, *Homily on the Solemnity of Our Lord Jesus Christ, King of the Universe*, 22 November 2020.

JOHN PAUL II, *Catechesi Tradendae. Apostolic Exhortation on Catechesis Today*, Vatican City, Libreria Editrice Vaticana, 1979.

JOHN PAUL II, *Familiaris Consortio. Apostolic Exhortation on the Role of Christian Family in the Modern World*, Vatican City, Libreria Editrice Vaticana, 1981.

JOHN PAUL II, Post-Synodal Apostolic Exhortation *Ecclesiae in Africa. On the Church in Africa and its Evangelizing Mission Towards the Year 2000,* Vatican City, Libreria Editrice Vaticana, 1995.

JOHN PAUL II, *To the College of Cardinals and members of the Roman Curia for Christmas,* 20 December 1985.

DICASTERY FOR LAITY, FAMILY AND LIFE, *Pastoral Guidelines for the Celebration of World Youth Day in the Particular Churches,* Vatican City, Libreria Editrice Vaticana, 22 April, 2021.

NATIONAL CONFERENCE OF CATHOLIC BISHOPS, *Music in Catholic Worship,* Washington, D.C. (1312 Massachusetts Ave., N.W., Washington 200005), 1983.

PONTIFICAL COUNCIL FOR PROMOTING NEW EVANGELIZATION, *Directory for Catechesis,* London, The Incorporated Catholic Society, 2020.

SECOND VATICAN COUNCIL, *Gaudium Et Spes. Pastoral Constitution on the Church in the Modern World,* Vatican City, Libreria Editrice Vaticana, 1965.

SYNOD OF BISHOPS, XV Ordinary General Assembly. "Preparatory Document" on *Young People, the Faith and Vocational Discernment,* Vatican City, Libreria Editrice Vaticana2017.

STUDIES

ALBERICH Emilio, *Catechesi e prassi ecclesiale. Identità e dimensioni della catechesi nella Chiesa di oggi,* Leumann (Torino), Elledici, 1982.

ALBERICH Emilio—Jerome VALLABARAJ, *Communicating a Faith that Transforms. A Handbook of Fundamental Catechetics,* Bangalore, Kristu Jyoti Publications, 2004.

ARKHIPOVA Elena, *Theory and practice of teaching the Russian language,* Moscow City, Routledge, 2009.

BRADFORD Brown, *The Science of Adolescence Risk-Taking: Workshop Report,* Washington, National Academies Press, 2011.

BUCKINGHAM David, *Is there a Digital Generation?* In Rebekah Willet (ed), *Digital Generations, Children, Young people and New media,* London, Lawrence Erlbaum Associates, 2006.

BUCKINGHAM David, *The Media Education Manifesto*, Cambridge, Polity Press, 2019.
COLEMAN John, *The Nature of Adolescence*, New York, Routledge, 1980.
DACEY John—John TRAVERS, *Human Development Across the Lifespan*, New York, McGraw-Hill, 2006.
FASICK Frank, "Parents, Peers, Youth Culture and Autonomy in Adolescence" in *Semantic Scholar* 1984.
FOWLER James, *Stages of Faith. The Psychology of Human Development and the Quest for Meaning*, New York, Harper One, 1995.
GROOME Thomas H., *Educating for Life. A Spiritual Vision for Every Teacher and Parent*, New York, A Herder & Herder Book, 1998.
GROOME Thomas H., *Christian Religious Education. Sharing Our Story and Vision*, California, Jossey-Bass Inc., 1999.
GROOME Thomas H., *Sharing Faith. A Comprehensive Approach to Religious Education and Pastoral Ministry The Way of Shared Praxis*, California, Harper San Francisco 1999.
GROOME Thomas H., *Will there be Faith. A New Vision for Educating and Growing Disciples*, New York, Harper One. 2011.
JACKSON Sandy—Luc GOOSSENS (edd.), *Handbook of Adolescent Development*, New York, Psychology Press, 2019.
MCDOWELL Josh—Bob HOSTETLER, *Handbook on Counseling Youth. A Comprehensive Guide for Equipping Youth Workers, Pastors, Teachers, Parents*, Dallas, World Publishing, 1996.
MEDDI Luciano, *Catechetica*, Bologna, EDB, 2022.
VALLABARAJ Jerome, *Faith-Focused Mentoring as a Paradigm for Youth Catechesis. Towards the Articulation of a Frame of Reference*, Bangalore, Kristu Jyoti Publications, 2012.

INTERNET SOURCES

AKIN Jimmy, "The Law of Gradualness," *Catholic Answers Magazine*, https://www. principle of gradualness, 13th October 2014.
ALLEN Brittany—Helen WATERMAN. "Stages of Adolescence," American Academy of Pediatrics, http://www.healthchildren.org, 28th March 2019.

Arkhipova Elena, "The Graduality Principle in Language Teaching," *The Linguistic and Didactic Aspects, Future Academy,* www.FutureAcademy.org.UK, 2nd February 2019.

Bill, "What is Art? *Artscolumbia,* artscolumbia.org, 2022

Harappa Diaries, "The Principles of Communication." *www.harappa-diaries.com,* 7th May 2021.

HASA, "Comic and Cartoon," *DifferenceBetween.com, 13th December 2016.*

Hoque Mohammad "Three Domains of Learning," *The Journal of EFL Education and Research,* Vol. 2, n. 2, *www.edrc-jefler.org.,* September 2016.

Maio Alyssa, "What is Comedy?" *StudioBinder, www.studioBinder.com,* 28th November 2019.

Mcleod Saul, "Erik Erikson Psychosocial Stages," *Simply Psychology, https://www. Simplypsychology.org/Erik-Erikson.html,* 3rd May 2018.

Miffleton Jack, "Music in Catechesis," *Oregon Catholic Press (OCP's Publications),* www.ocp.org, 26th November 2021.

Ruha Lily, "What is a Youth Festival," in *https://www.wisetour.com/what-is-a-youth-festival.htm,* 25th November 2022.

APPENDIX

SUMMARY OF KEY AREAS

GOALS OF FAITH EDUCATION (CATECHESIS)

- Communion with Jesus Christ
- Integral formation (subject matter of this book)
- Conversion
- Confession of faith in One God

AGE GROUP CATECHESIS

- *1–4 years: infants' catechesis*
- 5–9 years: children's catechesis
- 10–13 years: preadolescents' catechesis
- 14–17 years: middle adolescents' catechesis
- 18–21 years: late adolescents' catechesis
- 22–30 years: youth's catechesis
- 31–40 years: young adult's catechesis
- 41–65 years: middle adult's catechesis
- 66 years: late adult's catechesis

FOUR CATEGORIES OF CATECHESIS

- Children's catechesis (1–9)
- Adolescents' catechesis (10–21)

- Youth catechesis (22–40)
- Adult catechesis (41–)

NB. Adolescent and youth catechesis can also be jointly called *catechesis of persons in the realm of the young.*

The Three Domains of Learning

- Cognitive domain
- Affective domain
- Behavioral domain

Integral Dimensions of Faith Education

- Spiritual dimension
- Human dimension
- Intellectual dimension
- Apostolic dimension

Integral Tasks of Catechesis

- Promoting knowledge of the faith
- Liturgical education
- Moral education
- Teaching to pray
- Education for community life
- Missionary education

Perspective of Integral Faith Education

- Faith as believing
- Faith as trusting
- Faith as doing

INTEGRAL FAITH EDUCATION OF ADOLESCENTS AND YOUTH

Three Ways of Catechesis or Three "Hs"

- The way of the head
- The way of the heart
- The way of the hands

Pastoral Strategies in Youth Ministry

- Organic and structured catechetical programs
    - Development of the *kerygma*
        - Spiritual formation
        - Liturgical formation
        - Moral formation
        - Doctrinal formation
    - Growth
        - Fraternal love
        - Community life
        - Service
- Casual catechetical (formative) programs
    - Catechesis in institutions and associations
    - Catechesis in schools, colleges, and universities
    - Catechesis during pilgrimages
    - Catechesis during various events
- Vocational dimension catechetical programs
    - Priesthood
    - Consecrated life
    - Married life
- Youth culture catechetical programs
    - Music and catechesis
    - Comedy and catechesis
    - Movies/stories and catechesis
    - Cartoons/comics and catechesis

Two Main Courses of Action in Youth Ministry

- Outreach
- Growth

Faith-Focused Mentoring Holistic Approach

- Processes
    - Facilitating
    - Counseling
    - Protecting
    - Coaching
- Operational
    - It is developmental.
    - It is experiential.
    - It is integrative.
    - It is transformative.

Cornerstones of Every Youth Ministry and WYD

- Festival of faith
- Experience of the Church
- Missionary experience
- Vocational discernment and call to holiness
- Experience of pilgrimage
- Universal fraternity
- Youth festival
- Youth culture and *popular youth ministry*

Faith Initiation Process of Young People

- Socialization
- Evangelization
- Interiorization
- Integration

GUIDELINES OF EFFECTIVE FAITH COMMUNICATION

- The principle of clarity
- The principle of appropriate language
- The principle of attention
- The principle of feedback/human experience
- The principle of flexibility

ABOUT THE AUTHOR

Gatien Ngah is a priest of the Archdiocese of Bamenda, Cameroon, Africa. He holds a bachelor's degree in philosophy, theology, and educational sciences. He is a licentiate student in educational sciences with a specialization in catechetics at the Pontifical Salesian University, Rome. He has carried out research on faith education of the young in some communities in Africa, Latin America, Europe, and the United States. He has a five-year experience of working directly with thousands of young people in their process of faith education as chaplain. Gatien is the author of *Handbook for Altar Servers: A Compilation* (2017) and *Understanding and Living the Sacrament of Marriage: A Proximate and Immediate Preparatory Catechesis* (2021).

CPSIA information can be obtained
at www.ICGtesting.com
Printed in the USA
JSHW022110200723
45010JS00001B/6